On Women & Friendship

A Collection of Victorian Keepsakes and Traditions

STARR OCKENGA

STEWART, TABORI & CHANG

NEW YORK

Text and Photographs copyright © 1993 Starr Ockenga

Published in 1993 by Stewart, Tabori & Chang, Inc.
575 Broadway, New York, New York 10012

*When not otherwise indicated, items illustrated are from the collection of
the author. Measurements are in inches, width × height.*

Library of Congress Cataloging-in-Publication Data

Ockenga, Starr
On women & friendship: a collection of Victorian keepsakes and
traditions / Starr Ockenga
p. cm.
Includes bibliographical references and index.
ISBN 1-55670-242-6
1. Autograph albums – United States – History.   2. Friendship –
United States – History.   3. American poetry – Women authors.

This book, olden as it is, contains memory—living and refreshing—as they glowed in warm hearts.

4. Women – United States – History.   5. Women – Autographs
I. Title.   II. Title: On women and friendship.
Z42.4.U6025   1993
929.8'8'0973 – dc20   92-27152
CIP

Distributed in the U.S. by Workman Publishing,
708 Broadway, New York, New York 10003
Distributed in Canada by Canadian Manda Group,
P.O. Box 920 Station U, Toronto, Ontario M8Z 5P9
Distributed in all other territories (except Central and
South America) by Melia Publishing Services,
P.O. Box 1639, Maidenhead, Berkshire SL6 6YZ England
Central and South American accounts should contact
Export Sales Manager, Stewart, Tabori & Chang.

A Floyd Yearout Book

Printed in Singapore

1   2   3   4   5   6   7   8   9   10

To my sisters and soul mates
With thanks for the gift of their friendship

&

To the memory of the women whose names are recorded in this book.

Table of Contents

Introduction 8

LEAVES OF AFFECTION

The Handwritten Word 18

Printed Pages of Sentiment 46

Collections Between Covers 60

FRIENDSHIP KEEPSAKES

Tokens from the Heart 82

The Lasting Memento 106

Exchange of Likenesses 118

REMEMBER ME

To My Teacher 140

Hidden Languages 158

Comfort in Mourning 174

FORGET ME NOT

Appendix 196

Footnotes and Bibliographies 200

Index 206

A small memento left behind

Recalls an absent friend to mind

– M A R G A R E T

Angeline M. Graves' Album, 1838-1846

Perhaps I never would have assembled this material had I not moved. Establishing friendships in a new town is a slow process; as Sarah Josepha Hale wrote on March 13, 1843, "True friendship is no plant of hasty growth. . . ."

I was missing my old friends, and, as a collector, my personal preoccupations influenced what objects attracted me. I bought my first friendship album, a book exchanged among friends in the 19th century to gather their sentiments. I read the words from the past, from a way of life with a different pace, words from one woman to another about the meaning and importance of friendship. The women wrote of friendship as the staple of their lives.

Reading the messages from woman to woman, I became increasingly intrigued by the phenomenon of these books. While a few had been started by men, most had belonged to women. And most entries were written by women. Some were "schoolgirl-souvenir" albums, created to enshrine the friendships made at female academies. Used over many years, they recorded schoolgirl experiences, young teachers' work, marriages, the births and losses of children, the pleasure of the company of friends, and the loss of those friends. Even their own deaths were recorded in some women's albums.

Published history is usually about major events and the well-known figures who shaped them. This history is of a quieter sort. The owners of these albums wove the social fabric of an age, but very few of their names are remembered. The montage of words and mementos created by the last century's forgotten women have, for me, become a tender document of connections and feelings, as delicate and fragile as their braided hair wreaths. Viewed as a whole, the albums and related artifacts suggest a gentle but strong communion of women.

Nineteenth-century women were openly demonstrative about their affection, kissing each other on the lips when they met or separated, holding arms as they walked, speaking of their deep love in ardent terms. They were depicted in illustrations with that natural physical warmth, as in the engraving from a friendship album shown on page 9. *(American; 7 1/2 × 8 1/2"; Roberta Hansen Collection)*

Keepsakes of friendship exchanged between women took many forms, from poems recorded in albums to letters decorated with flowers. The symbol of clasped hands, meaning "hands in trust forever," is found on many objects, as is the request, "remember me." *(Cup: Patricia Byrne Collection)* The transcription of the page shown above, written by Sarah Josepha Hale, an influential editor of the period, March 13, 1843, reads: "True friendship is no plant of hasty growth / Though rooted in esteem's deep soil, the slow / And gradual culture of kind intercourse / Must bring it to perfection."

Among the many pleasures of imagination, none
exceed those arising from the memory of sweet
communion with those we love; and can the perusal
of a few lines written by a friend serve to call to
mind one passing recollection, the object of this
[book] will be accomplished.

Truly thy Friend

— SARAH HARTSEL, BERLIN, OHIO
Mahala L. Hartness Album 1860-1863

*W*omen were the keepers of domestic history. Their domain was
the home, and the preservation of
its day-to-day rhythm and special
occasions was their mission. By
tradition they were the creators of
the "remembrancers," and these
memorials took many forms. A
main focus of youthful education
was the making of ornamental
needlework pictures, or "samplers," depicting homes and families, with the inclusion of versed
sentiments of piety, family solidarity, and friendship.

Women kept track of past and current generations in
the family Bibles, often adding likenesses, particularly as
photography became accessible to the general public. A
few found time to write in journals, and many more chose
published prose and poetry to clip or copy and include in
their commonplace books. Perhaps they sensed they were
in a period of great change as the country shifted from an
agrarian society to an industrial one. Many were faced
with uprooting their families and moving across the country. Others stood by and watched as their sisters and
friends left for speculated opportunities in distant places.

*T*HIS HAIRWORK PIECE,
circled with the prevalent couplet
"The ring is round it hath no end
And so is my love to you my friend,"
was created by Lydia W. Eames
of Worcester, April 15, 1837.
(Catherine Scott Album, 1832-1839,
American; illustration: 1⅝" diameter)

Women wanted to remember their own histories and those
of their loved ones.

Women joined together to make gifts of love and com-
memoration, such as friendship quilts, and their backgrounds and cultures are pictured in the stitched designs.
Individually, they kept objects from weddings and funerals and turned them into memorials, artfully arranged in
shadow boxes, bell jars, or albums. In their leisure time
they recorded the beauty of nature around them in sketchbooks and herbaria and in their poetry. Pressed flowers
or sea moss, punched-paper book-
marks, and ribbons were slipped
inside the albums. Sometimes
friendship tokens were purchased
—giftbooks, jewelry of sentiment,
or whimsy boxes—but more often
they were made from materials at
hand. From all their domestic
handwork—the necessary linens,
bedclothes, and clothing—women
turned small scraps of fabric into
tokens of affection. These family
records, mementos, and memorials
to the ties of friendship were made to be savored in the present and saved for posterity.

I began to collect these books, and the piles grew; I borrowed from other collectors. I wanted to read a great many
in order to discover patterns and unique characteristics.
Each book represents a woman with a name, and each
woman was the center of a coterie of friends. Holding a
magnifying glass over faded handwriting, I searched for
clues to unravel the mysteries of these women's daily lives.
I worked alone for hours at a stretch, in my studio or in a
great silent library at Brown University, with just the

obligatory pencil to transcribe their words by my hand. I felt an almost physical connection as I touched the pages, keeping my place by running my finger along each line. The only sound was the rustle of old manuscripts as I slowly turned the pages. The bindings of these well-handled books are weak and must be handled with great care; that act alone reinforces the precious nature of each. Yet, poignantly, the women who inscribed them often referred to their "humble place" and the modest nature of the volumes. In gathering words and objects I hoped to bring the sweet voices of these women to life again; I wanted to know them better. Who were they and what were their real feelings about each other? Their language is sometimes painfully sentimental to modern ears, yet I found myself in sympathy with the formal tone, the dignity of their style of expression. Their writings, whether original or borrowed, mirrored their views of life. Their words, individual and collective, are a bridge back to the intimate circles of our foremothers.

It must be remembered that while most of the women who owned these books were of comfortable means, they did not control the family purse strings. Finance was the man's domain. Grand gifts from women to their friends were not only in poor taste, they were impossible to buy. So women who cared for each other demonstrated the depth of their feeling by creating small, personal, intimate tokens—a pressed flower tied with a silk ribbon or a lock of hair braided into a wreath and attached to an album with a tissue-paper heart no more than half an inch high.

I have chosen not to correct spelling and grammatical errors in quoting from the albums; they retain an authentic spirit when left as they were written. Wherever possible, I have recorded the full name of the author of a verse, but frequently the author signed with just her first name. I have tried to identify the albums' owners by name, although sometimes all I could find were initials. To the best of my ability, I have listed the span of dates during which an album was in use; however, so many entries are undated that no accurate picture of an album's active life can be clearly authenticated. Many may have been used for much longer periods than my dates suggest.

As I continued collecting, I discovered with considerable pleasure that I was entering an already well-established network of people engaged in preserving and protecting these endangered documents. Many of them generously opened their collections to me, believing that a broader audience would appreciate this fragile ephemera. Without their shared treasures and knowledge this celebration of friendship could not exist.

To Carrie

With fond affection true,
I write these lines for you;
By this token you may see,
I still remember thee.

—MARY F. TRAVER
Caroline E. Traver Album, 1852-1868
(Tobias Ricciardelli Collection)

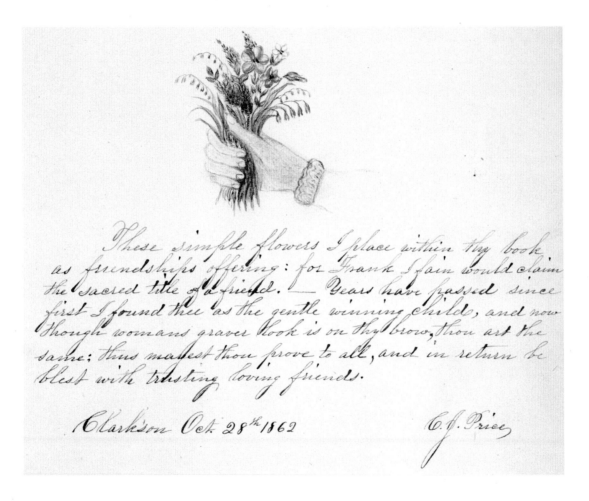

These simple flowers I place within thy book
as friendships offering: for Frank I fain would claim
the sacred title of a friend. —— Years have passed since
first I found thee as the gentle winning child, and now
though womans graver look is on thy brow, thou art the
same; thus mayest thou prove to all, and in return be
blest with trusting loving friends.

Clarkson Oct. 28th 1862   *C. J. Price*

THE SYMBOLIC HAND offering flowers is found in albums, on calling cards, and on friendship tokens. With the popularity of the language of flowers in the 19th century, often the tiny flowers were invested with meaning and could be read by the recipient as a distinct message. *("Frank" Album, 1861–1862, American; illustration: 1 × 1 ½"; Virginia Makis Collection)*

"Touch'd by the magic hand of those we love
A trifle, does of magnitude appear,
A pin, a fan, a blade of grass,
A bit of paper, then becomes most dear."

Henriett

Written album entries might be further personalized with pen-and-ink sketches or watercolor paintings, frequently of flowers. The rose's many varieties were a common choice. Yet each woman's version was unique, such as this theorem painting of the blossom's underside (above). *(Julia Van Dusen Album, 1829-1861, American; illustration: 2¼ × 2"; Virginia Makis Collection)*

LEAVES OF AFFECTION

The Handwritten Word

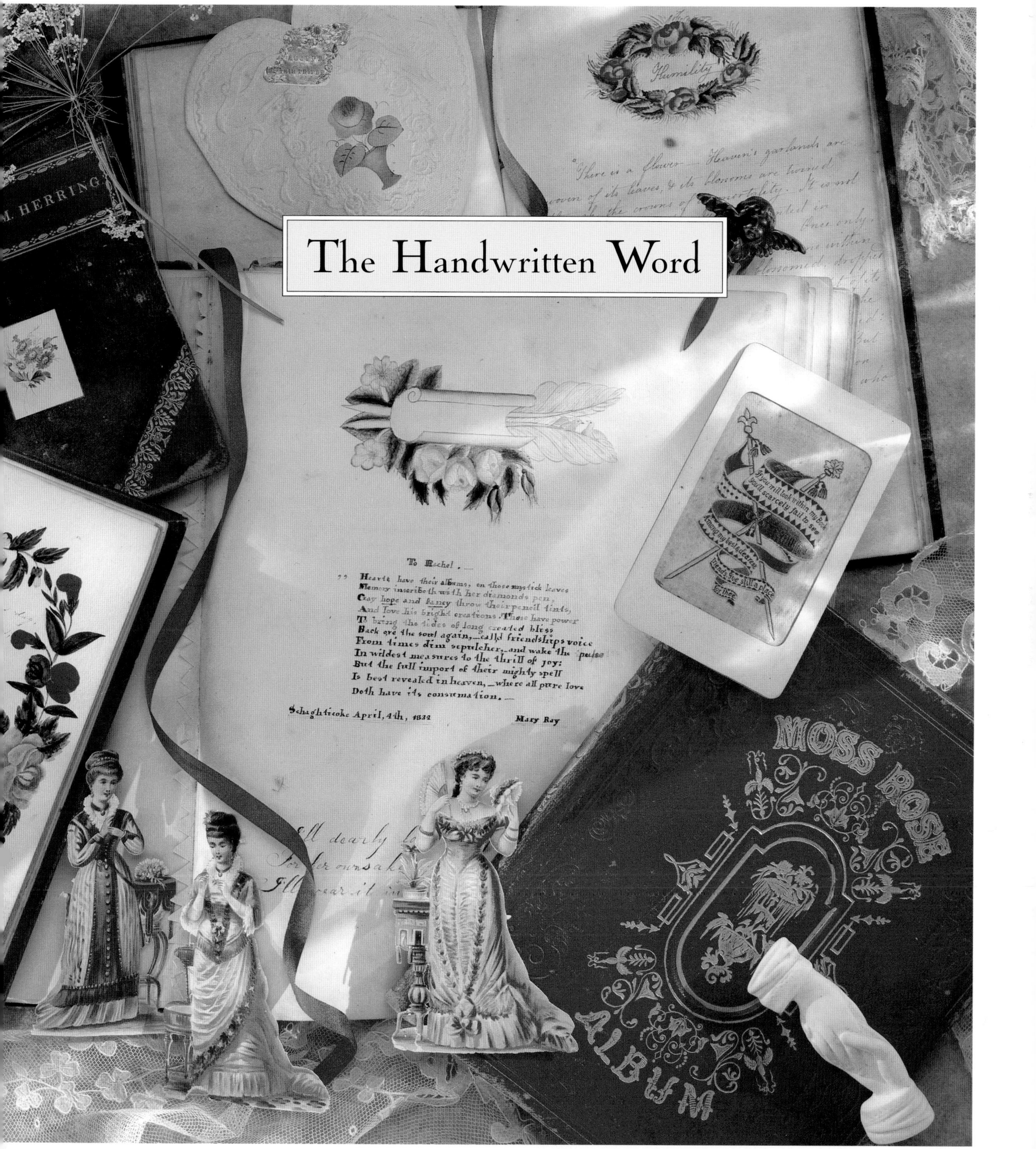

n 1829 Julia Van Dusen urged her friends to fill the "pure white" pages of her friendship album. Above her poem she sketched an open book, a facsimile of her own, with a quill pen by its side. In the mid-19th century many similar dedication pages were inscribed, as women on both sides of the Atlantic anticipated collecting goodwill and warm regards within bindings. ¶ In the role of "remembrancer," such a book was a repository of sentiments and tokens of affection, a shrine to the memory and pleasure of friendship. Most middle-class women owned one. Preserved over many years and surviving many moves, these books were reread for inspiration and solace, recording deep "sisterly affection" between women. Few other sources exist today that so eloquently outline the ordinary woman-to-woman relationships of that period. Filled with poetry (original and copied), watercolors, cutwork, newspaper and magazine clippings, and other mementos, they point to women's concerns and reveal secrets of their lives. ¶ Three types of these handwritten books endure. The friendship album—a book of entries by friends—is found most often. Second is the commonplace book, in which women saved favorite selections of poetry and prose, both their own and borrowed. The third and rarest group of these volumes are the journals, in which women described their day-to-day lives. Many handwritten books that survive today are a combination of all three.

THE GROUP OF AMERICAN friendship albums shown on the preceding pages date from the 1820s (Adeline Morgan) to the 1860s (album with tinted mother-of-pearl insets). All the paintings on the album pages are examples of hand-painted watercolors. Tokens of friendship, silk friendship cards, and hairwork are of the type found between album pages. The figures of women are die-cut scrap from the 1870s.

THE PORTFOLIO-STYLE album box (above) is filled with loose leaves in delicate colors on which friends have written messages. Also tucked between the pages in the box are pieces of hairwork, linen labels, and a friendship puzzle with the writing forming the shapes of leaves. Entries date from 1856-1870, and the towns are located in Switzerland. (Swiss; 3⅜ × 5¾"; Nancy Rosin Collection)

To M. C. Brooks

An Album is a thing of purity; a
Thing dearer than all earthly treasures;
It contains the best wishes of those We love
That in life's decline, we can look upon it
As a faithful and true representation, of
Our youthful and happy days. And as
We cast our eyes, over these pages
Stored with remembrances of the
Past, it is a solace which will
Bring us back, and add a
*   mitigating*
Balm in quiet reflection.
May this album be such to thee.

–THONDA
Mary Curtis Album, 1811-1852
(*Brown University Library*)

The most common subject of these albums is friendship itself, with attention paid also to piety, virtue, modesty, humility, religion, sympathy and mourning, and the love of nature. Authors often interwove these sentiments in a single piece. The cumulative content reflected the social attitudes and religious climate in which a woman lived.

In this period, a deeply religious culture dictated to women what they should believe and how they should behave, speak, and write. That they rarely deviated from those doctrines is obvious in their albums. Yet in spite of the severity and predictability of the language they used, an unmistakable sincerity emerges.

Friendship

Friendship is the affectionate unity, which exists between two or more, and endears them, to each other; by the strongest ties. There may be felt, in true friendship some of the most pure and disinterested emotions that this earth can afford. But we should be careful, and select only wise, and virtuous, for our companions; and put confidence in none, but those whom we have to be true, by a long acquaintance. There are many who are friends (or pretend to be) in prosperity but if adversity should visit us, will forsake us, and we cannot consider them, as real friends. It is those who will stand by us, in trouble, as well as in prosperity, who will sympathize with us, in affliction, and pour consolation into our bosoms, that we should prize above all others. That such may be yours is the wish of your sincere friend,

–HARRIET B. DAVIS
MINOT,
FEBRUARY 20TH, 1839
Elizabeth W. Chase Album,
1838-1839

Pages in friendship albums were decorated in a variety of ways, using the materials a woman had at hand. A silk ribbon, attached through slits cut in the sheet, was a frequent choice. On October 4th, 1829, Amanda Bryan chose a pale pink one to embellish her entry, shown opposite. (*Rachel Lownsberry Coryell Album, 1829-1841, American; illustration: 8 × 10"*) The engraving shown above was removed from an album. (*American; 6½ × 7½"; Bonnie Ferriss Collection*)

To Miss R Lownsberry

The fool may turn away
　　The bright eye hidden be
And tracts of earth unmeasured lay
　　Between thy friend and thee.

　Yet in communion sweet
　　'Mid contemplative hours
Congenial hearts as well may meet
　　As in their native bowers.

The parting pang may cost
　　A tear to dim the eye
And for thy form in distance lost
　　The yearning bosom sigh

But still our prayers may blend
　　From earth's remotest shore
While towards that holy clime we bend
　　Where partings are no more

Schenectady Oct th ... Amanda Bryan

for Mrs. Harriet Davis

On Friendship

Friendship I think is the choicest
flower that grows in natures
Garden it will always
flourish if waterd by
truth guarded by sincerity
And shaded by the
Gentle boughs
of virtue

Marcia M Marshall

A WATERCOLOR OF a weeping willow (opposite) encircles a poem on friendship. The album contains contributions from family and friends and poetic entries by its owner. It traveled with her from Grafton, Connecticut, to Canada, for her teaching sojourn, and back home again. *(Harriet Rider Album, 1835-1864, American; illustration: 5¼ × 7¾"; Nancy Rosin Collection)* The hand-colored engraving of a woman reading (overleaf) was probably tinted by the album's owner, an accomplished water-colorist. The subject of a woman reading, suggesting a love of books, was common to this album. *(Jane Allen Album, 1836, English; illustration: actual size; Cora Ginsburg Collection)*

THE ALBUM AMICORUM (above, left), a Dutch commonplace book, is engraved with the owner's name, Paulina Beljaart, on the front cover and the year of presentation, Anno 1798, on the back. All the poetic entries are written in the same hand. The latest date recorded is 1824. *(Album Amicorum, 1798-1824, Dutch; 7⅜ × 5"; Ursus Books and Prints, Ltd.)* A *Freundbuch* (above, right) takes the form of a portfolio box rather than a book, with individual leaves decorated with flowers and paintings as well as poetry. *(1820-1829, German; 6½ × 4⅛")*

You make a particular request that I shall write

on the first leaf of a book which you devote to friendship.

With solemnity of thought, fully aware of what I do, I write on the leaf.

There—it is done! What is done?

The league of friendship, existing before in spirit, is now in the letter also.

You are set apart from the world as respects me—I as it respects you.

If I am in need, sickness, or adversity, the world may pity,

but it is for you to relieve. If you are the victim of misfortune,

then it must be me to bring you relief and consolation.

This is not marriage; but it is something like it.

Mutually to love, to trust, to rejoice, to mourn together—

such is the relation which subsists between

Julia Pierpont Werne and Emma Willard.

— EMMA WILLARD

Julia Pierpont Werne Album, circa 1812

*E*lizabeth Chase's album is a schoolgirl's book. Often these albums debuted at the end of an academy experience, as many girls faced the threat of permanent separation from their classmates. Elizabeth and her classmates were influenced by one academy's philosophy, but their expressed sensibilities reflect those of the entire period. Written on the same day, in that same album, another entry reflects the humility ingrained in young women:

> *Miss Elizabeth, Agreeable to your request, I will endeavor to pen a few lines, for this little volume, however imperfect they may be. The thought intrudes itself, into my mind, that those pages may be filled with the productions of those who are better qualified to write, but the sentiments of the heart, I trust are not truer than mine. Though we may be separated, and perhaps you may never think, of your former associate M except while perusing these hasty lines, yet you may rest assured you will always be remembered by the subscriber;*

> – MARY L. DAVIS
> MINOT, FEBRUARY 20, 1839
> Elizabeth W. Chase Album, 1838–1839

*I*n reading their albums, it is tempting to speculate about these women, to let the hints and facts revealed suggest the details of their lives. Clearly, it is impossible to imagine the full picture behind the lovely old names—Hana Bigelow or Elizabeth Chase—but what emerges is a sense of their spirit and the value they placed on each other. In Harriet Rider's album, family members and friends penned entries of encouragement just prior to her move from the safety of her Grafton, Connecticut, home to assume a teaching position in "faraway" Canada. She, in turn, offered comfort to her nieces when they lost their mother (probably her sister), as glimpsed in the impassioned words of an elegy written in Harriet's album by one of the young girls. A newspaper clipping from April 18, 1870, titled "Romantic Marriage" and found in the album of Rebecca Jones from Cleveland, Ohio, reports an extraordinary tale of loyalty and fortitude. Her fiancé, "smitten with gold fever," left to make a fortune in the West. She remained faithful to him for 20 years, until he returned in "wealth and style" to marry her and escort her to their new home in Oakland, California. Her album exhibits the support provided by her friends through all those years.

Friendship albums were kept and entries made over many years. Numerous entries were not dated, and the breadth of an album's usage is frequently longer than can be documented. The first entry in Phoebe Nichols' album was made in 1837 and the last in 1901—a span of 64 years. Prized by their owners, albums were passed down to the next generation. Julia Van Dusen bequeathed her album to Julia M. Vaill, apparently her namesake, in 1865—36 years after the first entry was made.

At the end of Rebecca F. Gordon's album, in an insert written in a child's hand, Lewis Hall Gordon states that his grandmother's album was presented to him at the end of a four-month visit she paid his family in 1921. A fond relationship must have developed over that extended stay between Rebecca and her grandson (her husband's namesake) to precipitate her handing the album into his safekeeping. Perhaps the album, begun in 1852, was used as a memory reference for Rebecca to describe her girlhood surrounded by family, cousins, and friends, and to recall her courtship by a young man named Lewis Hall Gordon.

In an undated and barely legible entry on the last leaf of her album, probably inscribed many years after its daily usage, Rachel Coryell summarized its significance:

This book, olden as it is, contains memory—living and refreshing—as they glowed in warm hearts.

Rachel Lowensberry Coryell Album, 1829-1841

Through similar entries the common thread of women's warm friendship flows like a gentle breeze. Unlike the passion of male/female love relationships, these bonds are tender, described in delicate hands. They evoke pictures of women walking arm in arm, heads bowed in conversation.

Be assured, dear friend, Memory will never forget
The hours I have spent with you.

–CYNTHIA ANN
Mary A. Sawyer Album, 1829-1847
(Brown University Library)

Latin used by the scholars of the day. The fad spread from the Continent to England and Scotland. Students traveled extensively during that period, and a book of testimonials was valuable in gaining introduction to further social and academic circles. Goethe inscribed the initial entry in his son's book in the late 18th century. Translated, it reads:

Hand to the patron the book, and hand it to friend
and companion;
Hand to the traveler too, passing swift on his way;
He who with friendly gift, be it word or name,
thee enriches,
Stores up for thee a treasure of noble remembrance
for aye.[1]

The predecessor of the American friendship book was European—Dutch, French, and German—and was called *libre* or *album amicorum,* meaning, loosely, "book of friends." As early as the mid-16th century, university students, who were almost exclusively young men, carried small leather-bound books in which they gathered the approving thoughts of their patrons, teachers, and protectors, as well as their intimate friends. In fact, the word *amicus* also meant patron in the conversational

Later 18th-century examples survive, elaborately bound in baroque or rococo styles. The owners, by then young women as well as men, filled their pages with lines of original or copied verse. This sentiment-collecting developed, among some album owners, into a passion for celebrity entries and signatures. English poets Charles Lamb and Leigh Hunt, while denigrating the habit, wrote many entries themselves. Lamb even prepared what he called "advertisement verses" ahead of time, to be ready for young

$\mathcal{A}$BBA VOSE COLLECTED HER POEMS, composed over a number of years, and transcribed them into an album. Carefully written and illuminated in shades of red and blue ink, she signed the book with her own portrait inside a delicate wreath. She ordered her poems into two sections, one on childhood, where she wrote of her "maiden" dreams of buttercups and ferns, and the second on womanhood, where she celebrated the lives and mourned the loss of her children. *(Abba Vose Album, 1862, American; wreath and portrait: 3 × 3¼", title page: 6 × 7¾")*

 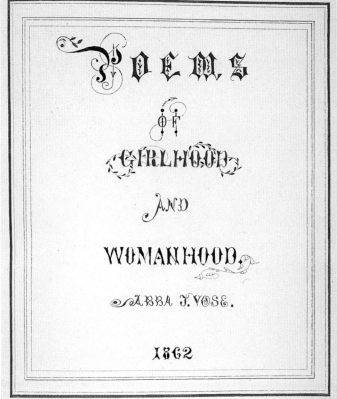

$\mathcal{T}$HIS SELECTION OF American albums (overleaf) is predominantly handmade, some with wallpaper bindings, some with newspaper leaves. Often the pages are almost entirely covered with attached newspaper clippings of poetry, enigmas, obituaries, or receipts. The woven heart is a valentine created from the cut strips of the leaves of a letter, thus implying a secret message of love. The tiny, blue silk heart outlined in ribbon contains the hair of a beloved brother. The watercolors are loose sheets found between album pages. All albums date from the 1840s and 1850s. *(Album in the foreground: Tobias Ricciardelli Collection)*

ladies' invitations. With an apt turn of phrase, he referred to the albums as "Gardens of wholesome herbs, Cabinets of curious porcelain, Chapels full of living friends, and Holy Rooms full of spirits of lost loved ones."[2]

The whiteness of the pages of an unused book was frequently viewed as a metaphor for the innocence, and presumed purity, of young womanhood. (The word "album" itself comes from the Latin adjective *albus,* meaning white.) Writing in the album of Lucy Barker, a Quakeress, Charles Lamb made the analogy:

> *Little book, surnamed of white,*
> *Clean as yet, and fair to sight*
> *Keep thy attribution right . . .*
> *Whitest thoughts in whitest dress,*
> *Candid meanings, best express*
> *Mind of quiet Quakeress.*[3]

The German name for these albums, *Stammbücher,* made reference to family, even to ancestors or roots. Traditionally a book was circulated amongst family members before being passed on to friends. Another early form, called *Freundbuch,* dating from the 1780s, was produced in portfolio-box style, with loose leaves to be filled in and returned to the box.

Because of the high cost of books and bindings at that time, most albums were owned by the well-to-do. It was in the 19th century that keeping a friendship album became a custom of the middle class, on both sides of the Atlantic. Early 19th-century American albums were blank books with simple board covers, often of marbleized paper. Sometimes the spines were leather, a style called quarter-bound; if leather corners were added, the book was termed half-bound. The albums ranged in size from folio to octavo, both vertical in format. The size in between, quarto, was more square in shape.[4] A number of albums from the 1820s

through the 1840s were handmade, sometimes with scraps of wallpaper as covers and newspaper as leaves. Their sizes varied from 10 to 15 inches in height to miniature versions just a couple of inches square. Often, in both the early hand and commercially bound books, the paper bore a watermark of the maker's initials and date. Holding the page up to the light reveals the impression, and the date of manufacture can be verified. Fine bindings were also sometimes privately commissioned. When a woman had accumulated a group of watercolors and writings by friends on individual leaves, she could preserve the collection by having it bound into book form.

English publishers, such as Marcus Ward & Company and W. & H. Rock, and American publishers, such as Leavitt & Allen, J. C. Riker, and T. W. Strong, soon discovered a broad commercial market for these books, and by mid-century they were producing elaborate albums with leather bindings decorated with blind and gold embossing, often including the owner's name. Elaborately decorated title pages read "The Young Lady's Remembrancer," "Album of the Heart," "The Lady's Tablet of Friendship," "The Gentle Reminder," or "Leaves of Affection." In 1860, G. G. Evans' Great Gift Book Store in Philadelphia listed 29 different versions of albums ranging in elegance and price. These books were embellished with steel and copperplate engravings of romanticized women in pastoral scenes or with flowers that invited hand-tinting by their owners.

The English and Continental commercial equivalents to American albums were considerably larger and more elaborate; in addition to leather bindings, they also included engravings. Some, like the "Album Orné," had ornamented empty frames on tinted pages for inserting art. Emulating British style, American publishers were quick to offer pastel-colored leaves and embossed borders as well.

An elderly contributor to the *Chambers Journal*, a British publication, for Saturday, August 30, 1873, remembered, "Those who can look back for half a century will remember the rage there was in their youthful days for albums . . . legion was not a name multitudinous enough for them; literary men crouched under their tyranny; young maidens wielded them as rods of iron. . . . Splendid books they were in their day, bound in rich morocco and gold, and often contained contributions from Scott, Moore, Montgomery and Praed; whilst Prout's beautiful sketches adorned their pages side by side with other artists."[5]

❋ While joy in relationships and awe or rapture at nature is prevalent in early 19th-century American albums, it is rare to find humor in the prose or poetry. The English, however, did indulge in mirth and satire, as evidenced by a

which *I* greatly lamented at the time, as *I* thought many persons might insert their contributions, and send me home, without being aware of what a magnificent thing *I* was: but this apprehension was totally groundless, for *I* never was in charge of any contributor, male or female, who did not, previously to writing, take off my silk dress to have a peep at the binding! *To* do them justice, however, they always replaced it so carefully that my mistress never conjectured *I* had been displaying my holiday costume.[6]

Whatever its form, from the most sophisticated bound volume to the smallest handmade book, the friendship album's intent remained the same: the passing on of affection and nurture from friend to friend. The authorship of most poetry inscribed in albums is obscure at best. Sometimes

Oft as you turn these pages o'er, And on beloved friends you sigh,

long piece in an 1831 English giftbook titled "Adventures of an Album." In it the album "describes" itself:

> *I am not one of the ordinary class of commonplace books of two-guinea value, to be found ready made and ready-faded at every repository of arts in the kingdom: no, I am an Exclusive, made in London for a lady who spared no expense to be considered one of the* elite *of a country-town. How much I was admired on my arrival!—and indeed I do not wonder at it, when I think of my splendid Burgundy-coloured binding richly gilt, and my pages of the purest white occasionally relieved by a tint of* coleur-de-rose, *which were preserved from the intrusive gaze of the unprivileged by a lock in the form of little-delicate hands. I soon had a crimson silk dress placed carefully over my beauties*

the contributor indicated that her poem was copied by writing that it had been "selected for" the album.

Well-known poets, such as Felicia Hemans or Henry Wadsworth Longfellow, might even be credited. Following a Robert Burns poem in one book, the inscriber wrote "countersigned by" before her signature. Lines composed by the author herself might begin with "original for" or simply "lines." But more often the origin is not clear; a poem might be copied from an obscure newspaper, a giftbook, or the monthly *Godey's Lady's Book,* or the verse was stored in memory and recounted on the album pages. Poems cut from periodicals are found slipped between pages of old albums, probably to be used as future inspiration. Frequently, words were crossed out and other words written in, suggesting spontaneous invention. However, in many cases, the perfection of the presentation suggests the author composed on a separate paper and then transcribed the finished piece into the book.

In a number of books pages are missing—if the artwork on that page was particularly charming it may have been removed to be sold separately. Dismantling albums is an unfortunate practice that is becoming more widespread. Pages were also eliminated when the albums were in use. When errors were made, the authors may simply have wanted a fresh start. To disguise a torn-out sheet, they cut a decorative zigzag pattern into the edge of the detached page. In *Adventures of the Album,* the album "reflects" on the behavior of one of the donors: "the . . . experiment was to cut out one of my leaves, in order to ascertain what sort of colours, ink &c. the paper would bear: and as this was the first wound I had received, it grieved me exceedingly; but I afterwards became more reconciled to such

Work even told the novice "how to sit at the desk and how to hold your pen."[8]

Many album pages are graced with watercolors of flowers, religious symbols, or motifs of virtue and piety. Some of the botanical paintings were rendered with skill and finesse. Brushes with only two or three hairs were used to execute the intricate detail, often accomplished with the aid of a magnifying glass. For those who lacked such talent, theorem painting, also called Oriental or Poonah painting, furnished a method of sure results. Using a series of stencils, called theorems, amateurs could paint flowers in baskets or vases with a distinct stylistic appeal. Occasionally, pencil or ink drawings of landscapes (in America, the dramatic shores of the Hudson River, and, in England, castle ruins) adorned the pages. By mid-century, as publishers began including engravings or lithographs in the

Though others may delight you more, Let mine not pass unheeded by.

treatment, and learned to consider myself very fortunate if the upsetting of the inkstand, or a bottle of velvet-colour, did not deprive me of three or four sheets."[7]

For most of the 19th century, it was expected that women could write with a beautiful hand. This tradition began in the 17th and 18th centuries and was more widespread in cultural circles in England, but it spread rapidly to America. To further decorate the page of an album, the author might write portions of an entry in Spencerian script with elaborate flourishes, or enhance the message with calligraphic scrolled drawings. By mid-century formal classes in this calligraphic art were being taught in the seminaries, and "self-instructors"—manuals in fancy pen-drawing—provided motivation and instruction on how to accomplish feats of embellishment with the tip of a pen. *Real Pen*

albums, women created fewer and fewer of these lovely watercolors. They continued, however, to paste decorative bits and pieces onto the pages, such as die cuts or portions of linen labels, tie pastel silk ribbons through slits incised in the page, or glue in cutwork wreaths and pin-prick flowers. A shared entreaty winds through all such entries: "Remember me," "Forget me not."

Remember me at twilight hour
When all around seems sweet & fair,
When mirth & jest have lost there power,
O, I would be remembered there.

– J. H. COLE
WINDSOR, FEB 2/60
Rebecca F. Hutchinson Album, 1852–1861
(Virginia Makis Collection)

*H*ANDWRITING IN ALBUMS and on friendship tokens and letters ranged from primitive script to fine calligraphy, as shown in these examples dating from the 1840s through the 1860s (preceding pages). The finely-wrought calligraphy piece on the left reads, "To Ellie, If sometime in pensive mood reclined, Your eye should wander to this page and see *M*y name with all these vines entwined, I will but crave one boon—*R*emember *M*e. Frank, Jan 1861, Phila." *(Two framed pieces: Nancy Rosin Collection)*

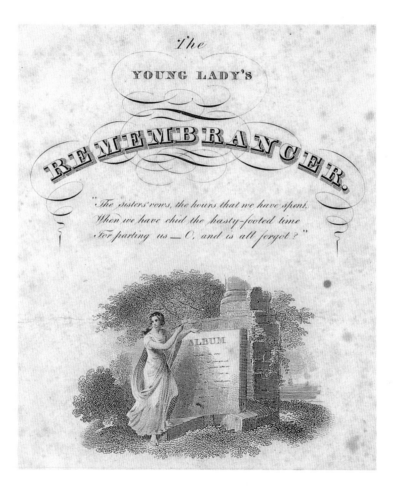

*F*RIENDSHIP ALBUM TITLES, such as the one above, reinforced the sentiments that were to be written on the pages. *(Rachel Lownsberry Coryell Album, 1829-1841; engraving: 2 1/2 × 1 3/4")* The poem opposite, written on a single leaf and given to a friend as a token of friendship, was personalized by woven hairwork and the common symbol of the double overlapping hearts. *(Sarah M. Shedd Letter, no date, American; 7 1/8 × 9 7/8"; Nancy Rosin Collection)*

Friendship.

"The world's weary pathway, we wander it through,
Some bright, glancing meteors ever in view,
And fair forms of fancy to beckon us on;
But ere we can grasp them, the charmers are gone.

As onward we hasten, new friendships arise,
To gild the dull moments of time as it flies;
But soon friends are parted, for transient are they,
And now are they severed and fled far away.

But friends once united in virtue and truth,
With all the affection inherent in youth,
Are not to be parted, by distance defined,
From those recollections that light up the mind.

For lovely as truly their images live,
Distinct as the pictures a limner can give —
Portrayed in such colors as never can depart
From Memory's escutcheon engraved on the heart."

Accept from one this lock of hair,
Who hopes your friendship ever to share.

Sarah M. Shedd.

Reading

As a rule, albums began with a dedication page, sometimes written by the presenter of the book:

The Album

Who will ask the utility of the Album? Who will say that these tender yet futile tributes are for nought? When days and years shall have passed, when many whose names are here enrolled shall be sleeping "the last sleep," as the fair owner of these tender mementos then reviews its fond pages, as she heaves the heartfelt sigh and sheds the sympathetic tear at friendships shrine, what heart so callous as then to say that all this is vain.

And, Rebecca, that the many kind wishes of these devoted friends may ever be realized that friendship such as is herin expressed, pure and unalloyed springing from the fountain of the heart may ever be yours is the sincere wish of

Your Sincere friend

– F. S. VAN ALSYNE
WINDSOR, NOV 25TH, 53
Rebecca F. Hutchinson Album, 1852-1861
(*Virginia Makis Collection*)

The interaction of families in small towns dominated the social life of the early 19th century, and many album entries were made by relatives. If the album was started when the owner was young, as was often the case, elders, including parents, aunts, uncles, and pastors, viewed it as an opportunity to give instruction, suggest etiquette, bestow wisdom and advice, and even to preach:

See to your book young lady, let it be
An index of your life—each page be pure

By vanity uncolored, and by vice
Unspotted. Cheerful be each modest leaf,
Not rude; and pious be each written page.
Without hypocrisy, be it devout
Without moroseness, be it serious.
If sportive—innocent. and if a tear
Blot its white margin, let it drop for those
Whose wickedness needs piety more than hate.
Hate no one—hate their vices, not themselves,
Spare many leaves for charity—that flower
Better than the roses first white bud
Becomes a woman's bosom. —there we seek
And there we find it first. Such be your book
And such, young Lady, always may you be.

– L. A. W.
WESTPORT, NOV. 30TH 1830
Mary. A. Sawyer Album, 1829-1847
(*Brown University Library*)

While most entries were written by women, a young man was sometimes confronted with a blank page. Embarrassed or shy as he might have been, he dared not refuse to make an offering. Pressured to produce an appropriate sentiment, his reluctance and fear of failure often came through in his entry.

Friendship's a name to few confined
The offspring of a noble mind
A generous warmth which fills the breast
And better felt than e'er expressed.

– EDWARD CROMWELL
Mary. P. Hull Album, 1834-1835
(*Tobias Ricciardelli Collection*)

In the January 1856 issue of *Godey's Lady's Book*, Mrs. C. W. Denison described the sorrows of a "poor young man" who was called upon to contribute to a lady's "cherished mental herbal." Suffering panic and writer's block, he dashed to the parlor library, and with "no need to improve on Burns, or polish Shakespeare," he "spread ambrosia in thin slides over the scented pages." All this to the great pleasure of his audience—the album owner and her friends—making him "fair game for matrimony."[9]

It became apparent that not only young men suffered from lack of inspiration, and publishers again hastened to answer the need. A range of "autograph writers," little booklets with paper covers, flooded the market. To attract males, some of the covers even pictured a man writing in an album, with the young woman owner watching happily over his shoulder. One published in 1885 was titled *Fifteen Hundred Selections in Prose and Verse for Autograph Albums.* Based on the already well-accepted style of "letter writers," it covered all the needs an author might encounter, from valentine messages to birthday wishes. This way, the owner was saved from the burden of having to be original.

Albums written in the form of diaries held especially personal thoughts and wishes. N. Baker of Woonsocket, Massachusetts, began her album on September 15, 1850, with a tender poem addressed to her husband, who had gone West to seek "the golden yellow ore." Three years later she noted that she and the children were "lonesome" but optimistic. On January 2, 1854, when she learned that her husband had died at Woods Diggings, California, Mrs. Baker entered a passage to his "precious" mem-

IN THE UNSIGNED EXAMPLE of microscopic writing above, the entire Lord's Prayer is written within a ⅞″ circle. (Julia Van Dusen Album, 1829-1861, American; actual size; Virginia Makis Collection)

ory. The last entry was dated 1866, 16 years after the album's inception.

Some women shared their diaries, revealing their joys and fears to intimate friends. The long tradition is evidenced in an 18th-century diary kept from 1754 to 1757 by Esther Edwards Burr. She lived in Newark in the demanding role as wife of the president of the College of New Jersey (later Princeton), and her journal took the form of letters sent at periodic intervals to her friend Sarah Prince in Boston. During an extended visit in Esther's home the two women formed a pact to write as confidants, primarily of their religious quest for deeper spirituality and, too, of their daily lives and feelings. It was not uncommon for Puritans to employ the journal as a means of self-analysis in the effort toward spiritual growth. Yet this partnership speaks of the sustaining power of the friendship between these two women: "for I look on the ties of friendship as sacred and I am of your mind, that it aught to be [a] matter of Solemn Prayer to God (where there is a friendship contracted) that it may be preserved.[10] . . . I have not one Sister I can write so freely to as to you the Sister of my heart."[11]

Mary Boykin Chesnut's entry for February 23, 1865, when her husband was away during the last weeks of the Civil War, reads:

Isabella has been reading my diaries. How we laugh. My sage ratiocinations—all come to naught. My famous insight into character—utter folly. They were lying on the hearth, ready to be burned, but she told me to hold on—think of it awhile. Don't be rash. . . . the 10 volumes of memoirs of the times I have written . . . still I write on, for if I have to burn—and here lie my treasures, ready for the

The Invitation

Come look at my Album but learn er'e you look

That all are expected to add to my book

You may quiz it and welcome the penalty is

You must leave a few stanzas for others to quiz

Or epic or epigramatic or lyric

With verses heroic, or verses satiric

If grave there's in all earthy volumes some leaf

Preserved for the sad overflowing of grief

If gay let your humour in poetry shine

And book it, yes book it and let it be mine.

– J U L I A

Julia Van Dusen Album, 1829-1861
(Virginia Makis Collection)

blazing hearth—still they have served already to while away four days of agony.[12]

Mary Chesnut was a prominent southern woman, and her diary, like others that contain facts and personal first-hand observations of a national crisis or event, have become primary source material for historians.

Because the creation of a poem or the execution of a painting took time, friendship albums were borrowed and taken to the inscriber's home. Other duties intervened, and often time passed before the album was returned to its owner. A poem published in *Peterson's Magazine* in 1855 records how this process could be somewhat stressful:

To Laura and the Album

Too long upon my table thou hast lain,
Thou "Moss Rose Album!" and it gives me pain
To send thee home, fearing thou wilt complain.

And yet I would have filled thy leaves with flowers,
Culled from the brightest beds and sweetest bowers,
Had not a thousand duties stolen all my hours.

So now return to Laura with a smile,
And tell her that I've thought of her the while,
With kindest love, though Duty did beguile.[13]

Commonplace books, mates of the journals, were used by their owners as treasuries to save poetry, prose, observations, and clippings. The term "commonplace" originally referred to a collection of writings on a general theme, but it evolved to encompass any subject that interested the compiler; generally the text was not original. Most often it was chosen from a variety of sources and copied into the album. Favorite English poets such as James Montgomery, William Cowper, Robert Southey, and Felicia Hemans were frequently quoted. Early in the century, many more English poets were excerpted than American, simply because they were more widely published in America. But as the century advanced, and more and more American poets were in print, Americans rushed, in nationalistic loyalty, to quote their own authors, with Lydia H. Sigourney as an often-represented songstress. Truisms of etiquette, riddles, enigmas, and conundrums were all included in commonplace books. From 1823 to 1834 Adeline Morgan entered poetry into a quarto-sized album. She chose subjects from "A Sister's Love" and "Absent Friends" to a celebration of "Bunker Hill." The book is filled from cover to cover in her deliberate and flowing hand, sometimes with more than one poem crowded on the page. With this book completed, she probably began another.

From the late 1870s to the end of the century, friendship albums and commonplace books show a shift in style and content. The emotional climate of the country was altered by the Civil War; sentimentalism in art and literature changed to a more realistic point of view, and that attitude filtered down to the way people expressed themselves. Albums became smaller, often horizontal in format, and they were generally termed "autograph books." The words "friendship" and "album" vanished from the bindings. The elegant leather and embossed bindings of mid-century disappeared. The entries became shorter—pat little paragraphs of well-wishing—and the charming watercolors all but disappeared. Autograph albums were still used by many women; the fashion had not died out. The custom simply seemed diluted, less personal, less passionate. A delicate genre of flowery remembrances had faded with age.

A MID-19TH CENTURY DIARY composed entirely in verse, letters, and a *Letter Writer,* 1845, are displayed on a desk top (page 43). The framed "*Star of Memory*" piece, created with cutwork hearts and woven hair, circa 1840, for Miss Jeanette Aldrich, reads, "When long years have passed away / Perchance these simple lines you'll see; / Then read my name here in the light / Shed from the *Star* of *Memory*." *(Nancy Rosin Collection)*

J.M. 1852.

*I*N ADDITION TO accomplished botanicals, women drew and painted exotic scenes of landscapes, frequently on a very small scale. The pen and ink drawing above, a gift to the album's owner, was signed and dated J. M., 1852. *(Sarah Ann Mandall Album, 1828-1852, English; illustration: 3¼" round)*

Printed Pages of Sentiment

ooks of friendship—lavishly bound and illustrated anthologies of prose and poetry issued each holiday season—became the rage of 19th-century gift-giving. A publishing phenomenon in both America and Europe from the 1820s to the 1860s, they are forgotten barometers of the popular taste of that era. ❡ America was in a period of peace and new prosperity. The country was changing from a primarily agrarian society centered around small towns to an industrialized nation with thriving cities. In swift succession inventions and discoveries such as the sewing machine, telegraph, telephone, and electricity transformed society. The population exploded with a great influx of immigrants hoping to take advantage of the reputed riches and opportunities. As education became more available to the general public, literacy increased. With the rise of the middle class, people looked for objects with which to beautify their homes and display their sense of style. Collecting became part of their consciousness. ❡ The desire for culture in the home quickly created a market for the elegant giftbooks; owning them was a symbol of a person's good taste and refinement. Americans were anxious to lay to rest their reputation as a young, riotous, even barbarian country of little force in arts and letters. They desired to read their own writers and see the work of their own artists. A national pride, if not a sophisticated level of discernment, developed for goods produced in America.

As with many items that were deemed "in good taste," giftbooks had their origin in Europe, in the 18th-century almanacs—little books filled with calendars, weather forecasts, and illustrations. Given as gifts, early almanacs were artfully bound, often with floral board covers, and slipcased (particularly those produced in France and Germany).

The first literary annual, *Almanac des Muses,* was published in Paris in 1765.[1] Most almanacs were small enough to fit in the palm of one's hand and were produced for feminine consumption. Even tinier versions of the almanacs were designed to hang on a chain around the owner's neck or be carried in an evening or dress bag. Thus the terms "ladies' books" and "pocket books" were coined. The more these almanacs were decorated with illustrations, poetry, and prose, the more popular they became, and the giftbook genre was born.

English publishers, noting the success of these books on the Continent, began to emulate their physical style and content. The publishers' efforts, begun in the early 1820s with titles like *The Forget Me Not* and *Literary Pocket Book: or Companion for the Lover of Nature and Art,* came to be known as "drawing-room annuals."[2] The fad quickly spread to America, (during the golden age more than sixty different titles appeared each year), not only with the importing of British giftbooks, which sold very well, but with the publication of *The American Ladies Pocket Book* and *The Atlantic Souvenir.* Because

women—"the arbiters of taste, and the ornaments of society"[3]—were the primary audience, giftbooks were designed to appeal to them.

Many carried expensive leather bindings, elegantly tooled and blind or gold embossed; others were bound in silk or velvet. Red, brown, and black were the favored colors, and endpapers were decorated with marbleized or patterned designs. Volumes generally began with an elegant presentation page, on which the giver was to sign his or her name, fill in the name of the recipient, and include appropriate sentiments. The inscription on the first leaf of a surviving copy of *The Lady's Gift* reads, "A Present from your friend, July 9th 1848. Remember the Giver."

Giftbooks were placed beside the Bible and hymnal on parlor tables and were often the focus of an evening's entertainment. Their poems and stories were read aloud to the family gathered in front of the fire. Women also read from them to their women friends over tea and needlework in the afternoons.

Many of these books were annuals, so when the new year's edition arrived, the old one was retired to the bookcase for future reference. Displayed for family and guests to enjoy, these books were the Victorian equivalent of today's "coffee-table" books:

To describe the delight of Amelia on receiving this elegant present is impossible. She spread a clean handkerchief over her lap before she drew the book

THE ARRAY OF American giftbooks (pages 46-47) dates from the 1830s to the 1860s. Placed on the parlor table, their prose, poetry, and "embellishments" provided the evening's entertainment around the fireside. The "To My Friend" bookmark is a Stevensgraph from England, circa 1880; the heart is a friendship token which opens into three hearts, each circled with poems of affection.

Early 19th-century French almanacs were produced as presents (preceding page). Widely popular, each small book (3 to 3½ inches by 4 to 5 inches), features delicate engravings, often hand-colored, some executed by the renowned Pancrea Bessa. *(Jutta Buck Collection)*

Book as necklace

from its case, that it might not be soiled in the slightest degree, and she removed to a distance from the fire lest the cover should be warped by the heat. After she had eagerly looked all through it, she commenced again, and examined the plates with the most minute attention. She then showed them to her little brother and sister.[4]

While there were many books published to attract the giftbook audience, the genre at its most pure is defined as a miscellaneous collection of prose and poetry, generally not previously published, assembled from a variety of authors. That they were intended as gifts was indicated by their titles—*The Gift, Keepsake, Token of Friendship, Memorial*—and often reinforced by subtitles—*A Christmas and New Year's Gift, A Gift for All Seasons.* Some subtitles were geared to attract the female audience by appealing to their sex, such as the none-too-succinct *An Offering to Beauty composed of the Choicest Descriptions of Female Loveliness, Virtues, Accomplishments, Attractions, and Charms; Comprising the Poetry of Women.* In a period when the symbolism of flowers and gems was commonly understood, some books bore titles such as *Moss Rose, Lily of the Valley, Forget Me Not, The Magnolia, The Garland,* and *The Pearl.* The average size of these books was approximately 5 by 7½ inches.

A whole range of miniature giftbooks (generally 4⅜ by 2¾ inches) flourished alongside the giftbooks, especially in the 1840s.[5] Not issued as annuals, they included selected poetry on a single topic such as friendship, the language of flowers, or mourning. Clothbound, with the only illustration a frontispiece, these were less expensive but charming versions of giftbooks, geared to the same female audience.

In the heyday of the giftbooks (the 1830s through the 1850s) their great attraction was the "embellishments," or illustrations, of which there were generally six to a dozen per book. Each "Publisher's Note" boasted of the high standards of the illustrations, most of which were steel or copperplate engravings made from original art. Both the artist and the engraver were credited. At the outset publishers often reproduced art that already existed, including the work of old masters, which they borrowed from collectors at little or no cost. When they did commission the work of American artists, such as Thomas Cole, Alvan Fisher, Henry Inman, Charles Robert Leslie, Thomas Sully, and William Sidney Mount, the mind-set for little remuneration was already in place. Conversely, well-established engravers, such as John Cheney and John Sartain, had already set standards for their fees, and they continued to be well compensated.

Appealing to the growing national pride in things American, some editors made particular note of the local origin. In the 1841 edition of *The Magnolia,* Henry W. Herbert wrote:

> *The engravings are, and will continue to be, executed entirely from American paintings, and by domestic artists—while no compositions, however excellent, will be admitted, which are not produced by writers, natives or residents of the United States.*[6]

With the invention of chromolithography in 1837[7], presentation and title pages became more ornate. Sometimes engravings of flowers were run opposite full-page illustrations. Usually hand-colored by the publisher, they varied in their degree of professionalism, according to the skill of the colorist. Occasionally, they were tinted by the books' owners.

The subject matter of the engravings complemented the text's artificial and romanticized themes—ladies, either in leisure and wealth or in abject poverty; utopian landscapes and seascapes; children in joyful or sad circumstances. Yet, for the period, their high quality was generally applauded by the audience, even by those who were critical of the text. Routinely, the engraving had been discovered or commissioned first and the author instructed to write to the image, rather than the reverse, so sometimes the engraving and the text were unrelated. With the advanced technology of steel-plate engravings, which replaced the earlier wood engravings, illustration was suddenly available at affordable prices to the general public, whetting a new appetite for art reproduction. Publishers were not above appropriating existing plates, particularly British ones, for use in their current editions. Repeated use of engravings from year to year and spurious borrowing were so common that some publishers took pains to assure readers that their new editions were above suspicion of previous usage.

Frequently, publishers also lifted their books' texts from other sources, even from other giftbooks, particularly after 1845. Purloined reprints, especially of British volumes, were notorious, as there were no American copyright laws for nonresidents until 1891.[8] (To the credit of the English publishers, they did not indulge in similar practices.) Sometimes a new annual consisted of the previous year's material with a new date or title, and even a new introductory poem, to fool the reading public. Occasionally, even the editors' names were appropriated. Greedy to capitalize on the success of giftbooks, publishers of monthly periodicals frequently rebound a year's issues as a unit and sold them as a giftbook, without any reference to their previous publication.

Most American giftbook publishers were located in the New England, New York, and Pennsylvania area, which was the primary seat of the market. Some of the more active were Carey & Hart of Philadelphia, publishers of *The Atlantic Souvenir* and *The Gift;* E. H.

Butler & Co. and J. B. Lippincott, also of Philadelphia; J. C. Riker, Leavitt & Allen, Nafis & Cornish of New York; Phillips, Sampson & Company of Boston; and Charles T. Gill of Nashua, New Hampshire. Many of these were also publishers of the friendship albums. They selected editors for their prominence and their reputations as arbiters of good taste. Many editors were men, but a significant number were women, a number of whom already had some reputation as poets.[9] Some of the books listed no editor, or attributed simply "A Lady." From all the editorial comments, both male and female editors were searching for the best writing they could find.

The popularity of the annuals spurred many people to try their hand at writing, and publishers were soon swamped with entries, especially of poetry. Some giftbook publishers offered prizes for the best entries, thus encouraging the better writers to compete. The prize money, ranging from $50.00 to as much as $200.00, was much more than the usual per-page payment of $1.50 to $3.00.[10] The first of these contests was held for *The Album,* in 1824. The resulting volume included the following, often-quoted lines in a poem titled "Address to the Album":

> Go! lovely volume—grace fair Beauty's bowers;
> Improve her heart—amuse her listless hours,
>
> Guide youthful Fancy's wild eccentric flight,
> Excursive through those fields of trackless light!
>
> Where bloom such flowers as deck thy glowing page
> With all the luxury of the golden age.[11]

Some of the best American writers wrote for the giftbooks. William Cullen Bryant, Edgar Allan Poe, Oliver Wendell Holmes, Nathaniel Hawthorne, Henry Wadsworth Longfellow, James Russell Lowell, Washington Irving,

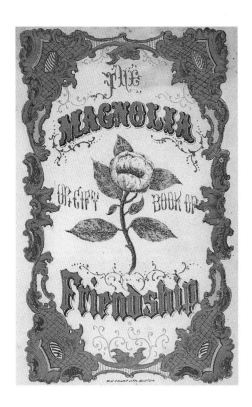 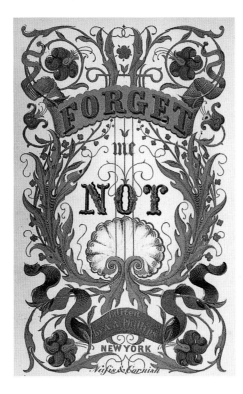 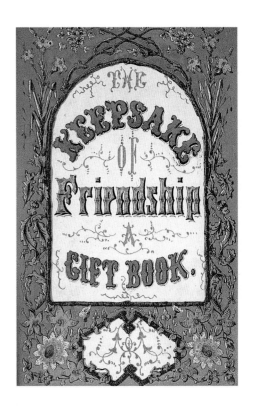

CHROMOLITHOGRAPHED title pages in mid-19th-century American giftbooks were highly decorative. The title page of "The Magnolia" was found with similar printed examples collected in an elaborate portfolio. *(Carol Greenberg Collection)* Publishers such as Nafis & Cornish of New York ("The Forget Me Not," 1849) and Phillips, Sampson, and Company of Boston ("The Keepsake of Friendship," 1855) produced elegant, if similarly conceived, versions as they competed for the primarily female audience. *(All books: 5 × 7½")*

and N. P. Willis were frequent contributors. Some wrote under pseudonyms in order to escape criticism about contributing to books of low literary quality. Only a few authors, like Walt Whitman, Henry David Thoreau, and Herman Melville, refused to write for giftbooks, although it is possible that their work also appears under pseudonym.[12] The books afforded women writers—such as Emma C. Embury, Sarah Josepha Hale, Frances S. Osgood, Catharine M. Sedgwick, Lydia Huntley Sigourney, and Harriet Beecher Stowe—publication alongside their better-known male contemporaries. The inclusion of their work in the giftbooks provided women with an important avenue into the field of American letters, previously dominated by men.

*T*he contents of the American giftbooks reflected the moral tenor of the time, with a concentration on beauty and an emphasis on character, virtue, and piety. Some, like *The Rose of Sharon,* one of the longest-running annuals (1842-1858), were outspokenly religious and spiritual in nature; many were actually edited by clergy, and ministers contributed prose and poetry.

America was used to directing its thought toward religion, and the religious and secular were frequently inseparable. Both popular literature and art tended to be sentimental, romantic, and exotic, rather than intellectual. It appears that since "the ladies" were the target audience, editors and publishers believed that it was the heart, not the

*G*IFTBOOKS WERE ALSO produced in miniature size (3 by 4½ inches). These smaller, less expensive versions were in vogue in the 1840s and 1850s. They were not published annually like their big sisters, but the topics were similar. Also shown are a framed friendship piece of clasped hands made of wax; examples of calling cards with a cardboard case in the shape of a book; and a vase of parian, or unglazed porcelain. *(Miniature giftbooks: Anchor and Dolphin Books)*

mind, they should engage. The language was high-minded in tone, and the subjects, besides the myriad approaches to purity and virtue, were home, marriage, travel, love of nature, preparation for death, mourning and the hope for eternal life, friendship, romantic and platonic love, and national folklore—particularly concerning Native Americans and African-Americans. In a young country developing a national image, there was a surprising lack of patriotism in this literature. The poetry was neither experimental nor strong, even at its best, and a great percentage of the prose, which was mostly fiction, suffered from the same limitations. Content was consistently serious, with the exception of a rare volume meant, perhaps, for a male audience. One stumbles on subtle wit in some pieces, but raucous humor had no place in books meant to elevate taste.

Some giftbooks were produced for a special occasion or a limited audience. When Frances S. Osgood died, her literary friends rallied to raise the money for a monument by compiling *The Memorial,* which was published in 1851. Several giftbooks were designed for brides, such as *The White Veil* (1854), edited by Sarah Josepha Hale. A number of volumes appeared with specific subjects, such as *The Temperance Offering* (1853), and *The Liberty Bell,* an antislavery annual published from 1839 to 1858. A whole family of language-of-flowers books were in vogue, often edited by the same group of women who produced the giftbooks. The Freemasons and the Odd Fellows were just

BOOKPLATES ARE as old as books, and have been
commissioned since the 15th century to mark ownership and insure
against loss and theft. Early plates were often depictions of coats of
arms, while others were unadorned, identified with only the owner's
name. By the late 19th century they were increasingly embellished
and personalized. The bookplate below left is American, drawn by
Sara B. Hill circa 1915. *(2 ¾ × 2 ⅞″)* The example to the right is
English and dates to the mid-19th century. *(2 × 1 ⅛″)*

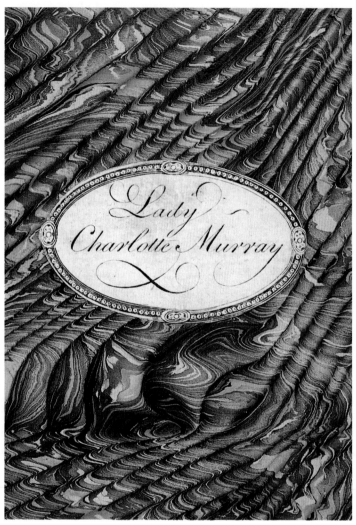

PUBLISHERS OFTEN embellished giftbooks with hand-
colored engravings, such as this frontispiece for *The Moss Rose*
(opposite). *(1849, American; 4 ½ × 7 ¼″)* Engravings were also
taken from other sources, hand-colored by the album's owner and
pasted into albums. The woman reading (overleaf) is from Jane
Ann Allen's album. *(1836, English; Cora Ginsburg Collection)*

a few of the societies that produced their own annuals. And there were also giftbooks specifically for children.

The demise of the giftbook coincided with the unrest that led to the Civil War. As the country's new problems set in, the economy tightened. Dreamy romanticism and sentimentality were no longer appropriate or marketable. More importantly, women began to take a different view of their roles in society. The suffrage movement began to take hold, and the suffragettes' convictions trickled down into average homes, affecting even those not actively involved in their cause. Newspapers and magazines, especially those geared to women, proliferated. Their costs were low and their subject matter current. Publishing standards and practices changed as well. With the introduction in the 1880s of binding machinery that allowed for mass production,[13] the giftbooks' beautiful bindings came to seem simply too expensive to produce.

Because of their sentimental nature, giftbooks have always been criticized for poor content, but there remains a certain grace and merit to these books. They are a document of the published literature and art meant for the female audience of the period, from 1825 to 1865.

This is what was available for average American women to read, and these books surely must have influenced women's attitudes and ways of expressing their feelings. Certainly they reflected strong feelings of loyalty and friendship. The nostalgia that the annuals evoke was perhaps best expressed by the editor of *The Laurel Wreath*:

An Annual is an offering at the shrine of friendship— a token of hallowed reminiscences that live and linger around the heart. . . . We hail these Annuals as the harbingers of better days. They help to feed the altar-fires of Friendship and bind the family of Man in holy brotherhood. If they do not embody the highest forms of literature, they yet speak the language of love, and afford the surest tokens of friendship— this makes them valuable. . . . So with the whole family of Annuals, while they are designed to be rich in poetry, thought, feeling, and sentiment; yet they are valued chiefly for the kindly emotions and cherished memories which they awaken. And when we find them on the center and parlor tables of our kindred and friends, we know that in every such family are the loved and valued—hearts, somewhere, that vibrate to kindred hearts.[14]

True Friendship

There are some spirits fitly strung,

To echo back the tones of mine;

And those few, cherished souls among,

I dare, dear friends, to number thine.

Angels attend thee; may their wings

Fan every shadow from thy brow;

For only bright and loving things

Should wait on one so good as thou.

And when my prayers are pure and strong,

As they in my best hours can be,

Amid my loved and cherished throng,

I then will count, and pray for thee.

– G . G .

Collections Between Covers

he passion for collecting flowered in the 19th century. As middle-class women had more leisure time and the world opened up to travel, Victorian ladies went on the hunt. At home and abroad they searched for treasures, from reproductions of classical busts and tartan boxes to a broad range of specimens from the natural world. ¶ The new amateur naturalists were especially passionate accumulators. They aggressively gathered, exchanged, or traded specimens such as bird eggs, fossils, butterflies, seashells, minerals, feathers, flowers, leaves, ferns, and mosses to display in the library, on the parlor walls, and even in their own rooms—and in albums. ¶ In 1855 Charles Kingsley wrote in *Glaucus; or the Wonders of the Shore,* "I have seen the young London beauty, amid all the excitement and temptation of luxury and flatter, with her heart pure and her mind occupied in a boudoir full of shells and fossils, flowers and sea-weeds, and keeping herself unspotted from the world, by considering the lilies of the field, how they grow."[1] ¶ Because of the social attitudes and restrictions prevalent in the 19th century, very few women actually became scientists. They were not expected to have careers, nor to exert their minds. Hugh Miller, a Scottish geologist, reflecting the general attitude of the era, instructed in a letter to his fiancée, "Oh my own Lydia, be careful of yourself. Take a little thought and much exercise. Read for amusement only. Set yourself to make a collection of shells, or

Ranunculus bulbosus.

butterflies, or plants. Do anything that will have interest enough to amuse you without requiring so much attention as to fatigue."[2]

Despite such advice, a number of women were serious about the study of natural history, and they left a rich legacy of information in their collections. Botany was a required subject of study in many female academies. Craving further knowledge, women attended lectures on subjects concerning the natural world, and courses were given and taken by women to pass on what they had learned. In their own parlors it was rare not to see a Wardian case of sealed glass displaying botanical specimens, or aquariums filled with samples from the sea. Among other items, shells, seeds, and feathers were crafted into stunning configurations and placed in shadow boxes or bell jars. Stuffed birds and animals were mounted in cases decorated to suggest natural habitats. *Art Recreations*, a women's manual of 1860, even provided instructions for women on performing taxidermy at home.[3] Whole rooms were dedicated to the preservation and presentation of collections, particularly those found in nature. Drawing and painting on their travels and in their gardens, women also produced fine collections of botanicals in their sketchbooks.

Albums became storehouses for specimens gathered from the natural world. The friendship album was, after all, a kind of collection—of sentiments in prose and poetry by friends. Adding the specimens from nature simply gave it another dimension. Some were plain, handmade books,

COLLECTING SPECIMENS OF nature was a passion of 19th-century culture (pages 60-61). Women ventured not only into gardens, but further afield into the woods and up mountains, preserving their prizes in albums of singular beauty. *(Tole vasculum specimen-carrying case: George Barlow Collection; "Ferns and Flowers" and "Souvenir 1859": Nancy Rosin Collection)* Using the Linnaean system of species description, probably learned in botany class, young women carefully arranged and labeled even the most common plants. *Ranunculus bulbosus,* or buttercup (page 63) is one of the 138 specimens in Rebecca Beach Judson's Herbarium. *(1840, American; 10½ × 16½"; Robert Fraker Collection)*

and others were ornate leather-bound volumes especially made or purchased to preserve a collection. By the 1860s publishers were producing books with "Herbarium" or "Sea Moss" embossed in gold on their covers. The young lady's manuals for deportment and improvement of the period lauded the study of sciences, including conchology, entomology, and mineralogy.[4] Armed with instruction manuals, and probably a certain amount of competitive spirit, young women searched for specimens.

A brook with banks of shells,
*   flowed through the grot;*
And oft the deer, amid the noon-
*   tide heat,*
Trooping to lave their lips in that
*   cool stream,*
Were startled by the student and
*   her lamp.*[5]

For amateur botanists, ferns and sea moss held romantic associations, perhaps because their habitats were more exotic than local gardens. Sea moss had to be pressed in an album, but a fern might be brought home roots and all, planted in a Wardian case, and nurtured, at least for a while, serving as a living reminder of a day's adventure. Fern collecting, or "pteridomania," was a remarkable fad in mid-century. Ferns of tremendous variety were sought, collected, exchanged, and exalted from England's forests, across America, to Australia and New Zealand. Shirley Hibbard, in *The Fern Garden* (1869), described ferns as "a sweet bit of vegetable jewelry" and "my plumy emerald green pets glistening with health and beadings of warm dew."[6]

To properly collect ferns and other botanical specimens, a tin container called a vasculum was *de rigueur*. It kept the specimens fresh for the trip home, where the plant would be pressed between pieces of rag paper and, when dry, transferred into albums. The owner labeled the plant, sometimes including location and date of discovery.

In addition to preparing specimen albums for themselves, women also assembled presentation books. Hannah Crawford Renwick titled hers *Ferns and Flowers from the Brisbane Water District* and gave it to her aunt, Mrs. Mary Carey. Using an elegant Marcus Ward & Co. Album from London, she compiled her labeled specimens into an enduring remembrance.

The allure of the sea and its rich offerings of colorful algae and mosses spurred many collectors, with petticoats

Each leaflet is a tiny scroll, ～ Inscribed with holy truths.

held high, to troop along the edges of tidal pools. Appearing in a range of greens, pinks, and reds, the bounty was especially rich when the tide was out or when a passing storm had detached and tossed the moss up on the shore. The author of *Art Recreations* effused:

> *The sea shore is an inexhaustible source of pleasure and instruction; and to one who has a taste for the beautiful, or who loves to search out the wonders of the ocean, and trace in them the footprints of the Creator, new avenues are constantly being opened for the acquisition of knowledge, and the means of rational and elevating pleasures.*

> *The great variety of sea weeds, their beauty and delicacy, and the graceful and attractive forms in which they can be arranged by skillful hands, have given to*

their collection and arrangement a deserved popularity among all frequenters of the sea shore; and it is a pleasant sight to see groups of children and adults, wandering along the surf-worn beach, selecting the delicate fringes of moss; and afterward, to see the fruit of their labors arranged in beautiful groupings, their bright colors well preserved, and the whole forming a picture pleasing to the eye and elevating to the taste.[7]

The sea-moss collector needed to carry a container of water in which to keep the moss fresh until it was laid out for mounting. Because it had to be pressed dry between blotter pages, moss was often arranged on small pieces of paper "relative to the size of the weed"[8] sometimes with a lightly oiled surface. The paper was slipped under the moss as it floated in its container of water, and lifted carefully. Next the moss was painstakingly spread out with a camel's hair brush or a pin and arranged into wreaths, flowers, or even baskets of flowers. Instruction guides advised, "Great care, patience, and delicacy of handling are necessary in this process, for much of the beauty of the specimen depends upon preserving the minute thread-like fibers of the weed."[9] Paper or linen was then laid over the top, and layers could be prepared in similar fashion until the whole stack was placed under pressure. Many suggested replacing the paper every two days with dry pieces. Portable presses were available to be carried out into the field, but most specimens were brought home for mounting.[10]

When the moss was ready, the tips were secured in place with gum arabic, and the arrangement placed in the album or framed and hung on the wall. Completed designs were often inserted into an album by slitting the album

*N*ot a tree

A plant, a leaf a blossom, but contains

A folio volume. We may read and read,

And read again, and still find something new,

Something to please, and something to instruct.

Given under my hand and seal,

Collectress of these plants.

—Rebecca Beach Judson Herbarium, 1840
(Robert Fraker Collection)

leaf with four diagonal cuts and tucking the mounting paper into these slits.

In her presentation volume of sea moss, Hana M. Bigelow penned an often-used poem:

Sea Weeds

Call us not weeds—we are flowers of the Sea
For lovely and bright and gay tinted are we,
And quite independent of culture of showers:
then call us not weeds, we are Ocean's gay flowers.

Hana M. Bigelow Sea Mosses Album, 1864

Another of the often-recorded sea-moss verses appears in an 1850 presentation album called Algae, given to Eliza Edgeworth Cary from Mary M. Chase. It reads:

Not fanned by the winds of a summer parterre,
Whose gales are but sighs of an evening air—
Our delicate, fragile, and exquisite forms
Are nursed by the billows, and rocked by the storms.

Mary M. Chase Album, 1850

In 1920, Maria Cary sent the album as a gift to her young cousins, Elizabeth and Caroline. Their father, she noted, was anxious for them to have something from their Chase ancestors. The "impressions," she wrote in a letter attached to the front leaf, "were taken in the season of 1850 when your Cousin Eliza spent the summer with her Aunt Mary, and together they studied field plants. Aunt Mary doing the indexing, and your cousin Eliza the stamping. The neatness and accuracy of the work has lost nothing by its seventy years. I can hardly hope to take care of them much longer, and I take real pleasure in passing them over to you." The pages of this album alternate between pressed

sea moss and the stanzas of a lengthy poem by Eliza Cook called "Song of the Seaweed." Poetry, and even drawings, were commonly added to the finished sea-moss arrangements. The center of a wreath of sea flowers seemed to ask for a piece of poetry or a sketch of a woman's face.

Gems of price are deeply hidden
'Neath the rugged rocks concealed;
What would ne'er come forth unbidden
To thy search may be revealed.

Moss Album, anonymous, 1863

In the herbarium or *hortus siccus*—a collection of dried botanical specimens in a systematic arrangement—meticulous identification of plants, including their Latin names, was common practice. Gathered from gardens, walks in the woods, and travels abroad, the plants were attached with tiny pieces of gummed paper which were sometimes provided by the publisher of the book. *The American Plant-Book* of 1879 boasted that "by the use of the gummed paper at the end of the book it is as easy to fasten a flower to its place, as it is to put a postage-stamp on a letter."[11]

In the rhetorical language of the period, Rebecca Beach Judson of Huntington, Connecticut, addressed an imaginary audience (probably never dreaming that some century and a half later she would have a real one) with a compelling and joyful invitation to experience nature and collect its bounty:

Gentle reader, art thou a botanist? I hope thou art!
But if it is not so—if thou perchance hast never with
scientific eye contemplated blossoms and plants, the
beautiful jewelry which garnishes the fervent bosom of
our common Mother Earth, then go forth with me
into the breezy fields; and as the young, joyous flowers

"No tale of love would I here breathe
Yet, my dear Geo, I fain would wreathe
A Sea Weed garland
        Whose leaves shall be
    Emblems and tokens of love to Thee —
Flowers! Oft bloom by the lowliest cot —
may They gladden & brighten & bless
                thy lot.

A RED LEATHER-BOUND ALBUM embossed in gold with
the word "Algae" on the cover was presented to George H. Rogers
on December 25th, 1848. Forty different configurations of sea moss
are carefully tipped in between tissued interleaves. The author of
the first page (above) remains nameless. *(George H. Rogers Album,*
1848, American; 7 × 4½")

To

My Mother.

Mother this book I dedicate to thee,
Thou who hast been all goodness unto me,
Accept this humble tribute of my love
All recompense from me thou art above.
Yet thou hast ever fondly smiled
Upon each worthy effort of thy child.

Rebecca

Huntington 1840.

ONE SPECTACULAR EXAMPLE OF the depth of
investigation and the flowery, descriptive language in this genre is
a volume "wrought" by Rebecca Beach Judson of Huntington,
Connecticut. Perhaps presented to her by her parents, the elaborate
leather-bound book is embossed with her name and the date, 1838.
She dedicated the book to her mother. *(Rebecca Beach Judson
Herbarium, 1840, American; 5¾ × 4¼"; Robert Fraker Collection)*

spring up around thy footsteps and balmy breath of Spring mantles thy cheek with a ruddier bloom, and causes gay hopes to efflores in the flower garden of thy heart, while radiant Health is joyously attuning thy bounding pulses; thou will be convinced that a study which calls forth such enjoyment is poetical! And albeit thou art no botanist, thou wilt grant in good sooth, ay, and feel too, there is poetry in botany.

Put on thy hat and gloves, and hasten with me, into Nature's brilliant emporium. What a perfumed, gorgeous Flower Fair, she is not holding forth 'neath azure, smiling skies, and golden, dancing sunbeams!

Rebecca Beach Judson Herbarium, 1840
(Robert Fraker Collection)

Rebecca Judson continued her treatise with many pages of handwritten and original text. Besides the excitement of collecting, she thoughtfully sought in nature the answer to larger questions of life:

It has not been mine to be deprived of many dear friends by death. But, one loved playmate of my school vacations, has bade me the long farewell. For me, now and ever, will the copse, the forest and the stream, we used to be happy in visiting,

Resound with a solemn, solemn tone, To me they'll speak of the dead and gone.

Dear Nancy Gibbs, thy fragrant memory can never be effaced from my heart's herbarium, where absence withers not, the divine flowers of friendship.

The theme of nature as teacher connects many of these herbaria. Another herbarium creator dedicated her book with the praise:

Day-stars! that ope your eyes with man, to twinkle From rainbow galaxies of earth's creation.

And dew-drops on her holy altars sprinkle As a libation . . .

Ye bright Mosaics! that with storied beauty The floor of nature's temple tesselate

With numerous emblems of instructive duty, Your forms create.

M. Louise Barron Herbarium, September 1856

The author of *Leaf and Flower Pictures, and How to Make Them* (1859) suggested that, in addition to labeling a flower in an herbarium, ladies also "write beneath it, the time when and the place where you gathered it. . . . Thus in a few years you will have a charming book, especially if you make it a rule to press at least one leaf or flower in every place you visit. Your Herbarium will then not only be a beautiful collection of lovely natural objects, but a mute remembrance of all the pleasant places you have visited and the pleasant people you have seen. Those who are fond of poetry, can write on each alternate leaf, any poetical description of the flower they have pressed, that they fancy."[12]

Memory bouquet albums, less scientific in impulse than the carefully labeled herbaria, also became popular for record-keeping. In 1859 two American women, probably the daughters of well-to-do parents, embarked on a grand tour of Europe carrying almost identical leather-bound albums, one deep maroon and the other brown with gold and silver embossing. The symbol in the cover's cartouche was a double harp, like that of the Gemini twins, holding suitable baskets of flowers.

On May 13, the two began their account with a visit to Le Havre, and over the next six months they traveled at an amazing clip through France, Belgium, Germany, Austria, Italy, Scotland, and England, returning to Italy to make the concluding entries in the Sardinian Alps on November 25. This trip may have been the final stage of the young women's education, or they may have been older women on a grand tour by themselves. In any case, it is easy to imagine these women clambering over ruins, picking and collecting flowers to press in their albums. The entries of both women on a particular date show the same varieties of plants, but in different configurations. What fun they must have had together! Did they both contribute

exhilaration of collecting and artfully preserving mementos discovered on such a journey. The plants are arranged like bouquets or celebratory wreaths on the pages.

Using moss on the title page, one woman formed the words "Souvenir 1859" and the other, "Flower Memories 1859." Conscientiously recording each site, from Napoleon's Tomb on May 23 to the Colosseum on November 5, they documented the progress of their trip and the flowers that grew at each stop. But, sadly, they did not record their own names.[13]

Another form of plant-specimen preservation was the taking of leaf impressions. Oiled paper was held in the smoke of a lamp until it became covered with soot. A leaf

to one large bunch of flowers to be divided back in their room, where they pressed and prepared them for albums?

They were particular in their choices, gathering small flowers that would fit well on the album pages. On July 31 in Martigny they found blue larkspur, and in Chamonix on August 1 they picked fern and white violets. In Strasbourg on August 9 they clipped fuschia, and on the 15th they discovered and picked English ivy growing on Heidelberg Castle. As the seasons changed, so did the flowers that commemorated the tour. The sisters were evidently familiar with botanists' techniques; the flowers were carefully pressed and adhered with tiny strips of paper. Their entries were not prepared with the precision of Rebecca Beach Judson's, yet they evoke the

was placed on the paper with its veined side toward the soot. Another piece of paper was placed over the leaf, and the resulting "sandwich" was then pressed with fingers or a roller. The blackened leaf, covered with a fresh piece of paper, was then pressed onto the album page and slowly lifted off, leaving a sketch-like "drawing" of its veins.

Butterflies were also conserved, not only in cases and specimen drawers, where they could be saved in their en-

THE TITLE PAGES (above), with letters formed from moss, are from two women's pressed-flower albums, created during their European tour in 1859. On September 8th each woman used similar specimens to create memory arrangements—a pressed basket and wreath—as their entries from Fountain's Abbey. *(American; both books 7¼ × 9¼"; Nancy Rosin Collection)*

tirety, but also in albums. One elegant, if tedious, technique for their preservation required laying the butterfly on a page and meticulously drawing its outline. The butterfly was then removed and the wing shape coated with a thin layer of liquid gum arabic. The wings were pulled off the butterfly with great care and laid on the outline, right side down. When the glue was dry, the wings were carefully removed with the blade of a knife, and as one manual described the process, "the down, or feathers" of the butterfly wing remained on the page "just as if painted; a perfect facsimile of the insect's wings." India ink or paint was used to fill in the body of the butterfly.[14]

The sketchbook was a frequent companion of Victorian women, both in their gardens and on holiday. Influenced by the English tradition of flower painting, American women also filled their books with drawings, watercolors, and gouache pieces. While romanticized landscapes of mansions, castles, classical ruins, glens, and idealized portraits of women and "exotics" were deemed correct subject matter, the most frequent and beautiful paintings were of flowers, from masterful renderings to simple, primitive representations. Tulips and narcissus abound, but the most popular flower was the rose—sometimes only an inch and a half high, other times larger, full-blown, and lush.

Like the specimen albums, sketchbooks became presentation gifts. A charming one, which includes some original and some selected poetry about flowers and butterflies, was made by J. E. Peabody. She identified each

---

To CREATE THE PAINTINGS that grace the pages of albums and sketchbooks, from the charmingly primitive to the more accomplished works, women used paint boxes, often well equipped (opposite). Both paintings in the frames are pages from albums. The theorem wreath of flowers is English School, circa 1830; the bouquet with a rose and tulip is American, circa 1820. (Ursus Books and Prints, Ltd.)

---

flower and often noted where it was found. Under her painting of forget-me-nots she wrote:

> Innocent children guileless and frail—
> Their meek little faces upturned and pale.

J. E. Peabody Album 1879
(Joseph Dermont Collection)

She presented her completed album to Cecil H. Peabody, perhaps her father or her husband, for Christmas in 1879 in Sapporo, Japan, "with much love."

 The all-inclusive word "scrap" defined another type of album. While some contemporary ephemera collectors use the term to refer exclusively to chromolithographed die-cut paper, in the 19th century, as today, scrap included all the precious paper treasures that were cut, borrowed, or saved from other sources and glued into an album. A very large (13½ by 10¼ inch) album inscribed in 1834 was designated by the owner on the opening page as a "Scrap Book," and spoke of the "great variety" to be found within its covers—engravings hand-colored by the author, cards, and original paintings. In the 1820s and 1830s publishers such as W. & H. Rock of London produced elegant, hand-tooled, leather-bound albums specifically for collecting scrap of this broader nature. Publishers did not generally distinguish whether the volume was intended for use as a friendship, scrap, or sketch album. The cover or spine might read simply "Album."

On January 22, 1832, at age 22, Sally Experience Brown began her diary, a day-to-day account of life in the Plymouth Notch area of Vermont. A single young woman, she was residing with her sister, as was often the custom, occupied in helping with the housework and the care of the children. In her journal's first entry she

An album given by Elizabeth "Lizzie" R. Blake of Philadelphia to Elizabeth "Lidie" B. Hayne, newly of Baltimore, features a number of drawings by an artist identified only by the intials J. E. B., probably Lizzie's brother. The drawings always include an initialed representation of the two young women, here the two swans. *(Elizabeth B. Hayne Album, 1828-1835, American; illustration: 3¹/₂ × 6"; Nancy Rosin Collection)*

Sarah Ann Mandrell's friendship album of poetry and painting contains a range of finely-rendered artwork (opposite), clearly not all illustrated by the owner, as the style varies from page to page. Among the works are a number of exquisite paintings of flowers, most of them unsigned. *(1832, English; clockwise from upper right: rhododendron arboreum, 3¹/₄ × 6¹/₄"; violets, 4 × 6"; Chinese vase of flowers, 2¹/₂ × 4¹/₂"; rose, 5¹/₂ × 6")*

Rhododendron arboreum
var fimbriatum

Sarah Ann
Mandall. 1832.

$\mathcal{A}$N IMAGINATIVE album owner trimmed pages in wallpaper and layered pieces cut from trade cards, greeting cards, and scrap to create a series of exuberant, colorful designs. *(Circa 1880, American; 6 × 7"; Elizabeth Baird Collection)* In another unusual album, innovative stage sets representing the rooms of a house were created on its pages (below, bottom). Curtains made of tissue paper, Dresden borders, and paper lace form the backgrounds for groupings of hand-colored paper doll-like figures cut from periodicals. *(Circa 1880; 6¾ × 8½"; Geo. Gregory Smart Collection)*

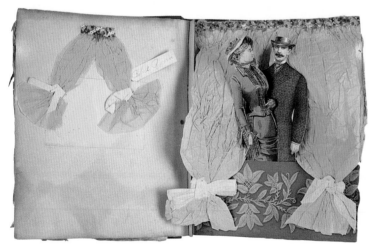 

$\mathcal{T}$HE SCRAP BOOK was a repository for collections of images on paper (overleaf). Early 19th-century examples contain engravings, often hand-colored, labels from fine products, valentines, and original artwork. As the century progressed, and lithography and die-cutting processes improved, these new images were assembled on the pages as well. This magnificent example begins with an address, dated 1834, playfully composed in the first person and signed by "The Scrap Book." *(Ursus Books and Prints, Ltd.)*

made reference to a "scrap book," clearly part common-place book:

This day (Sunday) commenced keeping a daily journal. James and Betsey went to a meeting at the Academy leaving the babe with me. I read some and took care of the children. Selected pieces for a scrap book.[15]

Scrap or "relief"—paper images die-cut or stamped, frequently embossed, and selectively gilded—began to appear with the invention of chromolithography in 1837. Initially manufactured in Germany, they were exported first to England, then to America. By mid-century and through the 1880s, scrap manufacturers in Europe, England, and America were flooding the market with these colorful images, and another craze was born. As printing techniques improved, prices dropped, making scrap more available to a larger audience.

Scrap was produced in sheets of similar images meant to be cut apart. Some included tributes, mottoes, and sayings of love and friendship. For valentine manufacturers the scrap was a boon, used to decorate otherwise white, lacy paper with color. Scrap allowed the buying public to assemble their own valentines or cards for special occasions, as well as to decorate the pages of their albums. Arrangements were sometimes made to form fanciful scenes, with birds and cupids flying, children playing, or bands marching, all surrounded by animals, butterflies, alphabet letters, buildings, or trees. Besides filling albums, these images also provided raw material for découpaged screens, trays, workboxes, needlework cases, and even furniture. Toward the end of the century, albums were so jammed with scrap that often no writing appeared at all.

The same printing techniques used to make sheets of scrap—chromolithography, relief-cutting or embossing, and gold leafing—were used for manufacturing labels for linens and other products. Colorful and collectable, these labels were often included in early albums. Later albums reflect the public's continuing taste for saving manufacturers' ephemera, as labels, tags, and trade cards were combined with scrap on the pages.

Albums were used for myriad purposes. Monograms cut from letterheads and calling cards became sought-after collectibles. Seeing a market for even this esoteric hobby, D. Appleton & Co. of New York produced "monogram albums," with gold-lined shapes printed on the page to receive the monograms. Unique albums were often devised by hand, such as a "house album," in which each room is represented by a stage set, replete with theatrical draperies and figures cut from periodicals. An entire book was made out of images cut from wallpaper and combined with advertising ephemera in collage fashion. Remarkable, surprising albums can still be found, evidence of brief trends or the product of one person's imagination. Behind each album was the desire to execute an idea or preserve the personal discoveries of the collector's whim within the bindings of a book.

Friendship

Friendship like an evergreen,
Will bear the inclement blast
And still retain the bloom of spring
When summer days are past

'Tis then true friendship ever lives
In hearts that are sincere
Unfading is the wreath she gives
It blooms throughout the year.

M. B.

Feb. 27. 1840

Forget Not Your Friend

FRIENDSHIP

Friendship

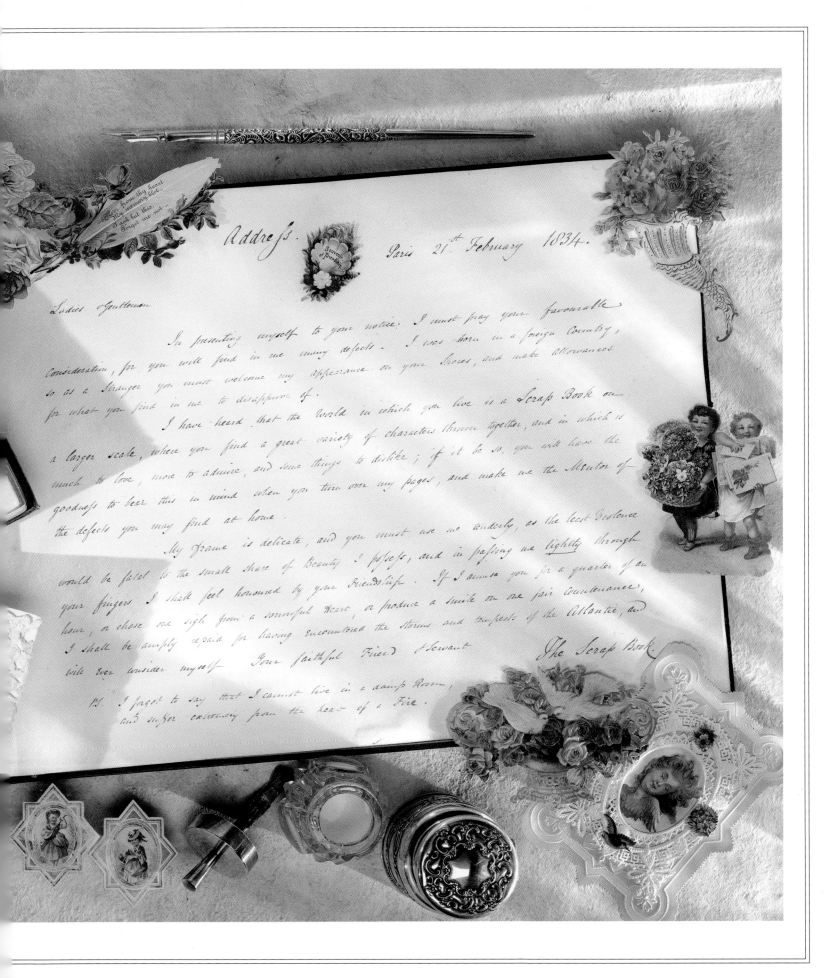

Address.   Souvenir of Friendship.   Paris 21st February 1834.

Ladies Gentlemen

In presenting myself to your notice. I must pray your favourable
consideration, for you will find in me many defects. I was born in a foreign Country,
so as a stranger you must welcome my appearance on your shores, and make allowances
for what you find in me to disapprove of.

I have heard that the world in which you live is a Scrap Book on
a larger scale, where you find a great variety of characters thrown together, and in which is
much to love, more to admire, and some things to dislike; if it be so, you will have the
goodness to bear this in mind when you turn over my pages, and make me the Master of
the defects you may find at home.

My frame is delicate, and you must use me tenderly, as the least violence
would be fatal to the small share of Beauty I possess, and in passing me lightly through
your fingers I shall feel honoured by your Friendship. If I amuse you for a quarter of an
hour, or chase one sigh from a sorrowful heart, or produce a smile on one fair countenance,
I shall be amply repaid for having encountered the storms and tempests of the Atlantic, and
will ever consider myself   Your faithful Friend & Servant

The Scrap Book.

PS. I forgot to say that I cannot live in a damp Room,
and suffer extremely from the heat of a Fire.

FRIENDSHIP KEEPSAKES

Tokens from the Heart

iscovered tucked into albums, giftbooks, and attic trunks from the 19th century are cherished trifles that women gave to each other in friendship. Forgotten for more than a century, these bookmarks and pincushions, needle cases and valentines, are artifacts of old networks of affection. Each object, however modest, is infused with the warmth of a cherished relationship. ¶ Many of these small gifts, stitched or embroidered, written or drawn, were made with the tools and materials most women had at hand. Some were purchased, but few were expensive. It was not the money spent that counted, but the sincerity of the love being passed on to a friend. The inscription "in sisterly affection" appears repeatedly. ¶ While perhaps only a small minority of young women were privy to *The Young Lady's Friend,* a book of advice written by "A Lady" in 1836, the author summed up the instinctive response of gift-giving of the period: "Always accept a present, however ill-chosen, in the same kind spirit in which it is offered; and never allow yourself to criticize or depreciate it. Let not your appreciation of a gift be according to its intrinsic worth, but according to the value of the sentiment that prompted it. Let the cheapest offering of a rich heart be honored, and placed among those of greatest price."[1] ¶ As needlework was an integral part of a woman's life from her early childhood, many of these tokens were made from workbasket scraps. (All clothing and household linens were sewn by

WHIMSY BOXES, TINY TOKENS of affection exchanged
at holidays or given at social occasions, held bonbons, a thimble, or
a handkerchief (preceding pages). Products such as powder, hair-
pins, or needles were packaged in charmingly decorated containers
intended to be reused or hung on the Christmas tree. Early in the
century they were made of cardboard with embossed borders, and
lithographed ladies graced the covers; later ones were made of
papier-mache, porcelain, or glass. *(Alice L. Kozlowski Collection)*

A RANGE OF TOKENS, a milliner's doll, and a whimsy
box on a lady's dressing table top (above) *suggest* small mementos
preserved for their sentimental meaning. The friendship cards
and the paper lace valentine, all mid-19th century, are typical of
ephemera exchanged between women to express their affection
for each other.

hand until the mid-19th century. Elias Howe invented the sewing machine in 1846, but it was at least another decade before its use became widespread in the home.) Very young girls learned to respect the needle's worth as they carried their precious needles back and forth to school, and were punished if they forgot them. Since great value was placed on needles and pins, appropriate receptacles for them were an obvious choice for gifts.

Needles—which in early times had been crafted of such diverse materials as thorns, fish and animal bone, wood, ivory, shell, gold, silver, bronze, and iron—were generally made of steel by the 19th century. If left out in the air they rusted, creating the need for small, airtight cases to protect them. Needle cases had taken various shapes over the centuries, from the lozenge-shaped or tubular holder hung from the waist to flat cases to be stored in a workbox. Every woman had her own needle case, whatever its shape, and it was often highly decorative.

Pins, too, were expensive and precious. Out of necessity to preserve these tools, women fashioned pincushions, or "pinpillows," in a variety of shapes and styles. Constructed from imagination or by following the proliferating designs in ladies' magazines, pincushions were the most popular needlework accessory of the day. From their workbaskets, using a scrap of dress silk, ribbons, or embroidery wool, women created these small gifts, sometimes personalized with the initials of both the maker and the recipient.

FRIENDSHIP QUILTS were made by groups of women to celebrate passages in their lives. Shown opposite are a "Friendship's Offering" appliqué quilt from Illinois, circa 1845, and a "Farmer's Bow Knot with Friendship Stars," dated 1891 and signed in embroidery with the names of the quilters (both, Laura Fisher, Antique Quilts and Americana). The pieced and appliquéd "Friendship Basket" quilt was made circa 1876 by the Devine family, owners of the local grocery store and post office in Stanfordville, New York, as a marriage quilt. (Tobias Ricciardelli Collection)

 Friendship quilts, formed by patterns of hand-sewn blocks, were textile versions of friendship albums. Each block was signed with its maker's name, and often with a date, location, and note of her relationship to the recipient, as well as poetry, messages, Bible verses, or sketches. Even the bits and pieces of cloth used were permeated with the memory of special dresses or events.

Unlike an album, which was inscribed by various individuals over many years, a quilt was made all at once to commemorate an event, celebrate a passage, create a memorial, mourn a separation, or record the names of family members or friends. Finishing the quilt was an occasion in itself, with each contributor stitching her part by hand. In quilt-making women gathered together to complete a gift of love.

> Great-Grandma made a "friendship quilt"
> Of scraps of calico.
> Her neighbors gave small bits of cloth
> From each new gown, and so
> Great-Grandma fashioned deftly
> A quilt of cheerful hues,
> And sewed with tiny stitches
> The pinks, and grays, and blues.
>
> —ELIZABETH CRAWFORD YATES [2]

The custom began in the 1840s and blossomed in the 1850s, as the expansion of cities and the westward movement threatened women with the possibility—and reality—of separation, and lasted well into the 20th century. Many of these quilts, testimonies of kinship and the bonds of friendship, were made for women who were taking leave of their homes and communities.

Women were used to identifying their household linens

by initialing, dating, and even numbering them with stitches, and they signed their textile gifts in the same fashion. Early inks contained ingredients that caused fabric to deteriorate and the signatures to disappear, but by the 1840s indelible inks were developed that allowed the signatures permanence, and those remain clear today. Women sometimes even used their own hair as thread when embroidering their names.

Looking at these quilts, deciphering their messages, and pinpointing the dates and places reveals secrets about the quilts' purpose and the owners' lives. Quilt collectors and historians speak of "reading" a quilt, for locked in those blocks and inscribed words is the love which women exchanged with each other. Pieced, patched, or appliquéd, they represent deep affection among women.

As a rule, a quilt is made up of three separate layers: the top, having been "set together," is the artful layer by which the quilt gets its name; the filling is cotton or wool batting; and the back is made up of lengths of yardage formed to make the size of the top. The earliest form of quilt in America was the one-piece quilt, in which all three layers were stitched together in a pattern or design. The patchwork quilt followed; created out of the scrap bag, it was a practical article of everyday use. Bits left over from making clothing or cut from worn-out garments were ingeniously pieced or patched together. New England—and even Virginia—winters were cold and houses drafty, so the frugal colonial women made use of every bit of cloth to create quilts to cover windows and doorways as well as beds. In use constantly, quilts tended to wear out; thus few early, utilitarian quilts survive.

A third type, called appliqué, was considered more ornamental than patchwork. Cutwork designs were stitched to a background, which was often white. The appliquéd motifs might be stuffed with padding to give them extra dimension. Sometimes all the blocks were the same size; other times a series of larger blocks were surrounded with smaller ones. A border could be added around the outside of the blocks, and the individual blocks perhaps separated by inserted strips of color.

To complete a quilt, of any style, a group of women worked at a wood frame prepared with the three layers—the top laid over the filler and the back. The gathering, called a "quilting bee," was a social occasion, an opportunity to exchange news, recipes, and remedies. At a typical bee, the women gathered early in the day, broke for a noonday meal, worked all afternoon, and then were joined by the menfolk and children for a special supper. Whatever the number of women assembled to work on the quilt, the evening was an excuse for a party.

With friendship quilts, the owner sometimes originated and organized the making of her own quilt. She asked friends to make blocks of a particular size, possibly even in a particular pattern. Custom required that these "memory blocks" be fashioned from the cloth of special dresses. Alternately, the quilt-maker might collect the favorite fabrics from her friends and make the blocks herself, or she

UNTIL THE MID-19TH CENTURY, dresses did not have attached pockets, but only slits in the skirts. Pockets, for carrying sewing tools and other necessities, were separate from the skirt, worn under it or attached to the waist. Handmade of fragments of muslin, linen, or calico, they were often created as a lesson in "plain sewing" in school. On October 21, 1820, Mary Underwood finished stitching a pocket of muslin and gathered it with silk ribbon. She decorated both sides with inked drawings and a poem called "Friendship," evoking "the heart to heart meeting in the bosom of a friend." It was dedicated and given to her mother. *(American; 9½ × 9½")*

might purchase the fabric, giving the quilt a more deliberate color scheme. Some women sent the completed blocks to their friends to be signed; others assembled the top, and then gathered her friends to sign it at the quilting.

In another version, a "Friendship Medley,"[3] friends of the (usually young) recipient all made blocks in different patterns, often appliquéd. Creating a medley called for two parties, the first of which was usually a surprise. At the first occasion, patterns were determined and the blocks completed and set together during the afternoon. Like the traditional quilting bees, these gatherings were filled with gossip, laughter, and quick stitching—an opportunity to show off one's needlework skills. Then the young men arrived for the evening's social activities, supper, dancing, and kissing games. The young recipient would give the

second bee, to which all the same friends were invited to quilt the medley of blocks.

Toward the end of the century, "crazy quilts," also called "puzzle patchwork," became the rage. Each block in these wildly-colored quilts was different, fashioned from velvets, silks, and satins in jewel tones. Those given in friendship carried signatures, often embroidered rather than penned. Unlike the more functional quilts, those created to commemorate friendship or events such as marriage were not used on a daily basis. Cherished, carefully stored, and displayed only on special occasions, many endure today.

There is a heap of comfort in making quilts, just to sit and sort over the pieces and call to mind that this piece or that is of the dress of a loved friend.

– AUNT JANE OF KENTUCKY[4]

Berlin Work embroidery, named for the German city where many of the patterns originated, became exceedingly popular in the 1830s and 1840s. A story, possibly apocryphal, is told that in 1804 A. Philipson, a Berlin printseller, and his wife began making paper with intersecting lines, similar to those on modern graph paper, which corresponded to the weave of a needlework canvas.[5] Motifs for needlework were first hand-drawn and then engraved on this squared paper, which was then sold for copying on to a canvas. The color schemes were thus predetermined, and the only choice left to the needlewoman was the background color. Although the level of creativity displayed in early samplers and needlework pictures was not as accomplished in Berlin Work, it did serve to make needlework design accessible to the rising middle class, lessening the necessity for strict needlework education.

Noting the success of these patterns, numerous other manufacturers, particularly in Germany and later in England, produced them in single-sheet style and, somewhat later, in pattern books of all sizes. Very few of the patterns were produced in America. Most Berlin Work was executed in cross- or tent stitch with the occasional addition of satin stitch. The patterns were easy to follow and

to transfer to the canvas attached to an embroidery frame. Early examples were executed in crewel or silk; the later ones, in wool. Manufacturers dyed wools in many gradations of color to enable the needlewoman to capture each nuance of the hand-colored patterns. Pillows, footstools, fire screens, bell pulls, and even slippers were decorated with delightful motifs of flowers, birds, animals, and borders. Some were copies of paintings, even rendering elaborate figural scenes depicting royalty (especially Victoria) or Biblical stories. As with all crafts, some Berlin Work was very beautifully rendered, and some was gaudy and graceless. They range from elegant, subtle floral pieces, embellished with stump work or raised work, to the ubiquitous framed mottoes claiming "Eternal Hope" or wishing "Good Health" or "Welcome" that hung over interior doorways in almost every home.

A simpler form of Berlin Work grew to fad proportions during the 1840s and 1850s, and continued growing until the end of the century. Called "punchwork," it was essentially Berlin Work done on perforated paper or on smooth laminated pasteboard, called bristol board, made of many layers of paper with tiny holes at regular intervals. The perforated paper could be purchased in various degrees of fineness. This craft did not require costly needlework canvas or time-consuming filling in of a background. By combining embroidery with lacy or geometric shapes cut out of the perforated paper, three-dimensional effects were created. The pre-drawn designs were often executed by schoolgirls, as the era of fine samplers and schoolgirl needlework came to a close.

With the rise in popularity of books and periodicals, punchwork bookmarks became perfect gifts of friendship. These small pieces were generally attached to a piece of colored, striped, or plaid silk ribbon. Mottoes intended for framing, calling-card cases, sewing boxes, letter folios,

and needle cases were given as trinkets. Personalized with initials and names, many also contained the language of symbols and flowers, allowing a specific message to be sent to the recipient. Crosses, anchors, and harps were surrounded with wreaths of flowers, and a number were finished with religious verses or words like "Friendship" or "Remember me." To further enhance the piece, the embroidery wool was sometimes embellished with beads.

By the 1870s perforated paper was manufactured in colors, including gold and silver, and designs were commercially printed on the bristol board itself, eliminating the need for pattern books, or for the inventive combining of patterns and alphabets. As with so many of these "fancy arts," punchwork was fresh for only a short period. When manufacturers commercialized the patterns, the charm and spontaneity of the earlier pieces was lost.

 Beadwork trinkets were immensely popular from the late 1840s through the turn of the century. They were crafted by women at home from the same patterns used in Berlin Work and punchwork, with monthly magazines such as *Godey's Lady's Book* or *Peterson's Magazine* providing additional designs and ideas. Made of silk, satin, cashmere, or velvet, and stuffed with combinations of cotton wadding, wool, bran, or sawdust, their charm depended on the abundance of the raised beadwork. A cut paper pattern was first sewn to the material and then arcs of thread, heavily beaded, were applied to the surface. These sometimes made the beaded design stand as much as half an inch off the surface. From the 1880s until 1910 Native Americans, bending to current Victorian taste, made vast numbers of these beaded souvenirs for popular consumption.

The boot, the strawberry, and the heart were fashionable shapes. Fancy beadwork took many forms: small

VICTORIAN PUNCHWORK or Berlin Work (preceding pages) was a popular means of embroidering small tokens of affection during the last half of the 19th century. Using perforated paper that simulated the texture of canvas, small mottoes, symbols, initials, and names and dates decorate bookmarks and card cases, often finished with silk ribbon. Patterns in single-sheet or book form provided instructions for the designs. *(Helen Walvoord Collection)*

VIGOROUS COLOR AND bold pattern distinguish both Victorian home-crafted beadwork and the Native American souvenir pieces (above). The difference between them is generally determined by the nature of the backing. The Native Americans used pink or flesh-colored, shiny cotton cambric, purchased in bulk particularly for that purpose; the homemade versions were backed with scraps and ribbons from the workbasket, giving a much more patched effect. *(Cecily Barth Firestein Collection)*

*E*UROPEAN EXPORTERS OFTEN enhanced their fine
silks and linens with labels with lithographed scenes of romance or
glorified portraits of women within gilded and embossed borders.
Some women collected these labels for inclusion in albums or to
decorate assembled pieces. This elaborate, mid-19th century
friendship token incorporates linen labels, cards, and hairwork.
Signed by Miss Margaret Plumber, it was probably made as a
memorial to a close friendship. *(American; 10 × 13")*

purses or reticules, watch pockets, wall pockets for collecting calling cards, pincushions, frames for photographs, eyeglass and scissor cases, and decorative pillows. The impulse of the gift was reinforced by the oft-repeated message "Think of Me."

Cutwork, or *Scherenschnitten,* a technique of cutting designs in paper with small, sharp scissors, originated in Germany and Switzerland in the mid-18th century. The craft quickly spread to America, particularly via the Pennsylvania German immigrants. Using strong, white rag paper, artisans cut designs freehand. They often folded the paper in order to duplicate patterns, which included love symbols such as hearts, wreaths, tulips, doves, and arrows. Messages honoring birth, baptism, name day, love, marriage, and death were written in careful penmanship and accomplished calligraphy, circling in and out through the bridges between cut shapes. Small examples meant as friendship tokens are found pasted in many surviving albums.

Another version of cut paper, called "papyrotamia," involved cutting complex scenes, rather than the more abstract motifs of Scherenschnitten. Ornately designed landscapes, complete with trees, birds, fences, and figures, or street scenes with buildings, coaches, and horses were cut and placed against a dark background. Still lifes displayed intricate floral designs or baskets of fruit. Sometimes they were formed in layers, creating three-dimensional effects. The process involved drawing a design in pencil on a sheet of heavy paper pinned to a board and using a sharp penknife to remove the larger blank parts. Then the paper was taken off the board and the more intricate trimming was done with special, extremely sharp, German-made scissors with long, thin blades.

A variation called "pierced paper," or "pinprick," entailed making a drawing using a system of dots and then piercing the dots with a pin. The dots drawn on the paper were so tiny that when the paper was pricked the dots disappeared, leaving an entirely white raised design, frequently in floral motifs. The paper was placed on a board or block, and the design was pricked, using pins or needles of various sizes, both from the front and the back, depending on where the creator wanted a raised or a recessed pattern to appear. The needle or pin was pushed into a piece of cork, forming a tool with a handle that protected the fingers. To produce variations in shape, slits, rather than holes, were incised with a razor-sharp knife or scissors. A technique called repoussé could be used to embellish the pinprick even further. The paper was wet from the back and then delicately stretched with the tip of a teaspoon or other rounded tool. When the paper dried, the back was reinforced with thinned glue to make it stiff. Finished pinprick designs could be tinted with watercolors.

The custom of sending cards or tokens—declarations of love—to a sweetheart or a special friend on February 14 is rooted in pagan rituals and feasts. Commemorating spring, love, and fertility, traditions from diverse areas have intermingled in the day named for St. Valentine, the patron saint of lovers. Valentinus, a Roman priest who gave aid and comfort to Christians during their persecution, and who subsequently was converted to Christianity, was executed for his faith on February 14, A.D. 270. In the legend, his last gesture was to send a letter to his jailer's daughter, a young girl whose sight he had restored, signed, "From your Valentine." After his death a pink almond tree—a symbol of abiding love—grew and flowered above his grave in a churchyard in Rome.[6]

Coincidentally, the ancient Roman feast of Lupercalia, a fertility revelry sacred to Faunus, or Pan (the god of

To Miss Mary A. Sawyer

They say that Friendship's but a name
A vain and empty sound;

Has thou ne'er felt its influence,
A faithful friend ne'er found:

Upon whose breast you might repose
The burdens of your care;

Whose faithful heart with yours would feel;
And every trouble share:

And when the tempestuous tide ran high;
Would love you to the end,

If not, accept my heart
In Friendship's strongest Tie;
And in Friendship let us die.

Accept this dear Mary, as a Tribute of
Friendship, from your friend

– CAROLINE C. HALSTEAD
WESTPORT [CT], MAY 29, 1830

Mary A. Sawyer Album, 1829-1847
(Brown University Library)

A Gift of St. Valentine

flocks, feeder of herdsmen), was observed on February 15. The association of St. Valentine's name with the festival came about by the accident of time. Brought to Britain during the Roman occupation, the ancient rituals evolved with gentler observances and the holiday developed into a predominantly Anglo-Saxon celebration, spreading from England to America, and becoming particularly observed in the 19th century. The warmth of feeling it inspired was not limited to exchange between lovers; friends and relatives also took the opportunity to express their affection.

Paper tokens with verses date from the 15th century. Printed valentines, produced first in Germany and then in England, were originally reproductions of woodcuts; engravings and then lithographs, often hand-colored, followed. Some designs featured open areas in the center in which the sender could write his or her own message.

The earliest American valentines were handmade, handsealed, and hand-carried to the door of the beloved. By 1845 uniform postage rates were established, and the sender was able to use a prepaid mail system through which envelopes were stamped with a postmark, most commonly an irregular red circle enclosing the words "Paid 5."[7]

Early American valentines, dating back as far as the mid-18th century, took various styles. Some were drawn and painted on leaves of paper, others used the Scherenschnitten or papyrotamia processes, and most employed careful, if not elegant, penmanship. Poetry and messages of devotion were also written on decorated paper, which could be purchased from stationers and printers. Verses of romantic poetry or word puzzles such as cryptograms or rebuses (where some words were represented by drawings), or acrostics accompanied the designs. Sometimes folding the paper would create a puzzle called a puzzle-purse. By opening it, unfolding it, or turning the paper and reading around in circles, the message became clear. Popular lines became valentine vernacular: "Let us join hand and heart, never to part." "Valentine writers," small books of verses, aided those to whom poetry did not come easily. They were published in England and imported to America as early as 1723.[8] But these were rare and many of the poems on early valentines are original or, at the very least, were passed on by word-of-mouth. Often early valentines were intended by shy swains as proposals of marriage.

While not as delicately made, some late Victorian valentines, exchanged from the 1880s to the turn of the century, are extremely decorative. Ingeniously constructed, they open, hang, or stand. Ornamental boxes enclose layers of lace and lithography or open like elegant little books; cards unfold to reveal elaborate three-dimensional scenes of airplanes, roadsters, arches with garlands, or cherubs offering bouquets of flowers; and fans spread out to spell "Offering of Friendship."

Used during the same era, and paralleling valentines in style, were a myriad of calling cards. Purchased directly

THE 1880s STAND-UP English valentine opposite depicts two women together, a frequent theme in Victorian valentines, as they were often traded by women. Chromolithographed, die-cut, and heavily embossed, it was addressed to "Sister." The dresses, a revival of Grecian style, are in the tradition of the Aesthetic Movement. (5½ × 9¾"; Nancy Rosin Collection) The late-19th century paper tokens (page 97) include an advertising fan from the New Home Sewing Machine Company and cards printed by Raphael Tuck, an English manufacturer. On the blue fan, a souvenir of a Watermelon Feast on August 25, 1893, all the guests have signed their names.

from salesmen or through stationery shops, they were exchanged and collected by the millions. Initially, the cards were printed in black and white and then hand-colored by the purchaser. Many bore little poems of friendship. Later examples were decorated with pieces of "scrap," the colorful chromolithographed die cuts. In a variation called Hidden Message Cards, the scrap could be lifted to reveal the sender's name or message, which created a sense of mystery. Accordion-shaped salesmen's sample books provided an array of choices for the consumer. The cards were elaborate and colorful, flowery in motto and verse, and playful or ardent in intent. Used to send messages in floral language, symbols, rebuses, and puzzles, "calling" cards appear to have been a national pastime.

Other paper tokens, varying in expense and quality, also came into vogue. Charming lacy cards pledged "Sincere Affection" or "Friendship's Tie," while paper hearts opened to be filled with flowers, or fans revealed poems of friendship. Since fans were part of a woman's accessories, they were especially fashionable as friendship mementos and provided a natural place to collect signatures, particularly at a party or dance. And by the late 19th century, advertising ephemera became so alluring that many women collected and exchanged pieces, often gluing them into friendship albums.

Puzzles and games, sometimes more playful in their sentiments than cards and favors, were also kept in the albums. In endless knots of friendship, trails of writing carried the verse through a maze. The reader could start at the beginning, where the writing trail entered the knot, or pick up and read at any place throughout the design, twisting and turning the paper to decipher the message.

Acrostics—poems composed so that the first letters in their lines, when read vertically, spelled out the name of the recipient—provided means of personalizing the verse.

To aid the author, if inspiration was lacking, paper booklets were published offering acrostics for the common first names of women. However, since the custom seems to have called for using both first and last names, most verses were original. Spelling out "Julia Kent," a friend wrote:

An Acrostick

Joyous was the news when thou wert born.
Unfading brightness tinged the rising morn.
Life-light and glory hovered round thy head.
Infantile reason op'd thy eyes and shed
A glorious lustre around thy infant bed.

Knowledge gigantic now surrounds thy youth.
Enrich'd with virtue and eternal truth.
Noble in mind thy genius soars on high.
Through realms of wisdom teach the young to fly.

– E. B. HUBBARD
ALBANY JUNE 19TH 1829
Julia Kent Van Dusen Album, 1829-1861
(Virginia Makis Collection)

*F*riendship could also be pledged in a puzzle form in which each intersection of connecting shapes was meant to reiterate the vow of constancy. In the friendship's wreath seen here (page 101), it is pledged 112 times by overlapping hearts, circles, and squares. The poem following the puzzle is entitled "Friendship's Pledge":

But few the flowers that friendship wreathes
To seal her sweetest vow,
And few the words the minstrel breathes
A Pledge is Friendship now.

And as these Squares, howe'er you read
To Friendship pledge, I vow

Friendship's Wreath

Friendship is here pledged 112 times.
Begin at the left & right hand, & at the top & bottom of the Squares; & at any word on the four Circles, Curves & Hearts, & read both ways.

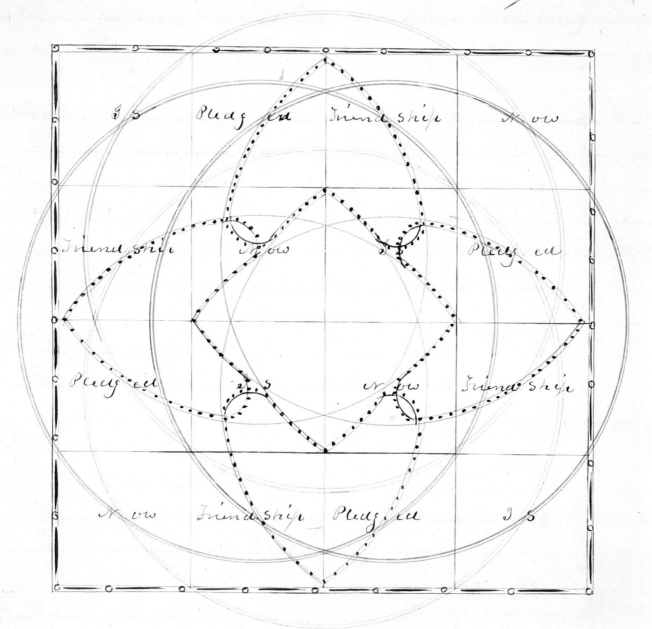

Life's checkered scenes will ever lead
To Friendship pledged as now.

Hearts linked to hearts and bound by ties
That speak of Friendship's vow;
A stronger symbol art denies
Than pledges Friendship now.

Circles, that never, never end,
And Curves bind firm the vow;
As through life's varying
scenes we send
Be Friendship pledged
as now.

Your friend

– M . B . S E A R S

Perhaps the most accessible keepsakes that could be purchased in the mid- to late-19th century were pieces of inexpensive "jewelry of sentiment." Made of nonprecious stones and materials, such as aluminum, steel, jet (and its substitutes, bog oak and gutta-percha), some were love tokens, some, memorial pieces, but many were given in friendship. They might be personalized with a woman's name, or offer "Gratitude" in raised relief.

Since sentiment and symbolism go hand in hand, each motif on this jewelry had a meaning. The cross stood for faith, the anchor for hope, the serpent for eternity, and the tree for life. A variety of love and friendship motifs, such as the heart, clasped hands or the single outstretched hand,

bows, the endless knot of love, pairs of doves, and cherubs carried messages. The language of flowers—ivy for friendship, the forget-me-not for remembrance—appeared on many pieces. Royal symbols such as the crown were fashionable, particularly in England and especially to commemorate Victoria's jubilees—her 5oth in 1887, her 6oth in 1897—and then her death in 1901. The word "Mizpah," engraved on many pieces of the jewelry, was in such vogue that it also appeared on printed paper, bookmarks, and other ephemera. From a quotation in Genesis, it means, "The Lord watch between me and thee when we are absent one from another." Bristol glass, porcelain cups, and plates that spoke of friendship could also be purchased inexpensively and given as gifts. These, like the jewelry, might include a name or the words "Friendship," "Forget Me Not," or simply, "A Token."

As with all of these charming objects, the most special and touching are those made by a woman's hand, with simple materials left over from other tasks. Personal and intimate, they are fragile reminders of strong relationships.

Jewelry of sentiment, small and generally inexpensive, was filled with symbolic meaning (overleaf). Ivy, horseshoes, hearts, and doves and the words "Best Wishes," "Mizpah," or the name of the recipient might be incorporated into the pin or locket. When enhanced with semiprecious materials like agate, ivory, or coral, the jewelry became especially colorful and decorative. Some contained locks of hair, particularly those worn as memorial pieces. *(Jean Berger Collection)*

Friendship

To Miss Elizabeth Morrison

Breathed from the lips of friendship, take my warmest wishes for thee,

Thou charming, bright and fair, thou long mayest to be,

That thou mayest still retain thy power through every coming year,

To friends, and all, day after day, more valued, loved and dear,

And with the treasures of the mind mayest thou pure, innocent and gay,

Cherish those feelings of the heart that never know decay,

Whilst meek religion to the soul, the sweetest solace given,

Shall yield thee happiness on earth and point thy steps to Heaven.

Accept the wishes of thy friend.

Endless Knot of Friendship, circa 1840
(American; 5½ × 5")

The Lasting Memento

Preserving the hair of loved ones has been a sentimental custom for centuries. Most commonly the hair, a simple lock or several strands arranged to form decorative braids, feathers, or flowers, was crafted into a piece of jewelry or carried in some other token chamber as a reminder of a distant or deceased loved one. This tradition blossomed during the 18th century, as hair saved in a pendant, ring, or brooch could be worn, like a talisman, close to the heart. ¶ In the 19th century saving hair evolved into a fad, peaking in the 1840s and 1850s, and enduring until the 1880s. Hair art, once mounted only by professional jewelers into love tokens and memorial jewelry, began to be the work of the amateur, and most of the homemade hairwork was produced by women. "If I should from this world / Depart you'd have a bit of my / Heir my hand and heart if we / Could no more each other see / You could still remember me"–Ann Elizabeth Brugh, January the 16 1853. *(Sarah Brough Braid Album, 1846-1853; Joe and Honey Freedman Collection)* ¶ Albums, the standard treasury of memory and memento, were already becoming popular as early as the 1820s. By the 1830s tokens made of hair, intimate and personal, became familiar gifts friends could present to friends. "When this you see, remember me," was a common and moving plea. An added fragment of ribbon made a charming and individual prize, a gift that would last forever. Importantly, too, this keepsake required no money to purchase. Once again,

*I*N THE MIDST OF A SELECTION of mid-19th century hairwork (preceding pages) is the family record book of Jane P. Bierle. "Commenced" on January 4, 1853, she attached twelve woven, twisted, or braided pieces to each page. On the single leaf in the box, under Miss Mary Ann McGuyre's name, are four lines: "Oh, my friend? I never, never / Shall forget to think of thee / And I hope that thou wilt ever / Midst thy joy remember me." *(Joe and Honey Freedman Collection)*

*T*HE GARDNER FAMILY BOOK (1867-1898), was probably made by Mercy W. Gardner (above). Within, scrap, labels and clippings hold the hair in place. In the upper left, Lydia J. Ensign's book (1840-1848), lies open to the dedication. The book in the upper center, begun on February 22, 1842, belonged to Louisa E. Ensign, probably Lydia's sister, as both books were found together. One can imagine the two girls working on their hair books side by side. *(Joe and Honey Freedman Collection)*

lack of control over money influenced the development of simple tradition:

> 24 January 1862
> . . . why feel like a beggar, utterly humiliated and degraded when I am forced to say I need money? I cannot tell, but I do; and the worst of it, this thing grows worse as one grows older. Money ought not to be asked for, or given to a man's wife as a gift. Something must be due her, and that she should have, and no growling and grumbling nor warnings against waste and extravagance, nor hints as to the need of economy, nor amazement that the last supply has given out already. What a proud woman suffers under all this, who can tell? And one thing is sure, nothing but the direst necessity drives her to speak of deficit—empty purse . . . What a world of heart burning some regular arrangement of pin money must save.
>
> —MARY BOYKIN CHESNUT[1]

This lament, while not always expressed so eloquently, must have been deeply felt by multitudes of women across the nation. Yet out of the constraint of no coins in their purses evolved much of the folk art—primitive, naive, and pure—that historians and collectors value today. Thus, of necessity, many of the tokens exchanged could not be "dear."

The religious climate of the period was also influential in the growth of hairwork as an art form. With the swell of spiritual fervor, a preoccupation with the temporal nature of life, the inevitability of death, and the philosophy of dust to dust, only one's hair would last beyond the grave. Human hair does not decompose. While heaven was the understood goal of life's journey, and poem after poem writ-ten or copied by these women attests to that belief and acceptance, there is also a passionate, often-repeated desire not to be forgotten. Women wanted to leave something tangible behind. The exchange of hairwork mementos offered promise of immortality in a very mortal world:

> Our life's a narrow span
> A short uncertain day
> And if we reach the age of man
> It soon will pass away
>
> —BUSHY, BROUGH FAMILY HAIR PIECES, JAN. 12TH 1846
> (Joe and Honey Freedman Collection)

Many friendship albums included hairwork pieces, as well as the more typical watercolor paintings of flowers. Generally, these pieces took the form of braids or wreaths of one person's hair, tied with a silk ribbon and either sewn or pasted to a page. In addition, whole albums were dedicated to hairwork. The vernacular terms "hair books," "hair albums," or "braid albums" define the bittersweet genre:

> Sarah Brough her braid Album
> Comensed Jan 12th 1846
> When this you see remember me.
>
> Sarah Brough Album, 1846-1853
> (Joe and Honey Freedman Collection)

While some of these hair records were created in albums with fine bindings, others were made in simple copy books, perhaps by young girls as school projects. More often the albums were handmade, with bindings of cardboard covered with wallpaper, calico, or even silk. Individual leaves were sewn in place, and ribbons might decorate the binding or form a closure with a button or bow. The albums ranged

Money lament (handwritten margin note)

in size from 3 by 4 inches to 8 by 10 inches, or even larger. Since paper was precious and not to be wasted, rarely did these handmade books reach the size of the commercially available albums. The care that went into creating them was testimony to the significance that the collections had to their owners. Direct and unaffected, they stand as a compelling personal art form.

Sometimes a hair token lay alone on a page, and in other cases as many as 10 to 12 were arranged together. The backs of the sewn pages are designs in themselves, random—almost modern—patterns of dark thread fastening the hair to the reverse side of the sheet. The inclusion of a cutwork heart or hand, a linen label, a face or figure cut from a periodical engraving, a scrap of ribbon or a piece of a dress, enhanced the presentation. Almost all hairworks were identified with the owner's name, and sometimes the relationship to the album owner (father, mother, cousin, friend) was noted. These small mementos of hair marked the presence and celebrated the existence of each person.

Occasionally each piece was dated, but often not, although the album owner might have recorded the date when she "commenced" it. When a whole album was dedicated to hairwork, it appears that the owner herself collected and crafted the pieces. Conversely, when a hair token appeared on the page of a friendship album, it was made and placed there by the author of the inscription.

(Joe and Honey Freedman Collection)

Some hair albums were created to document the genealogy of a family, taking the place of a family tree or family record. Made by the women, they disclose another example of women's efforts as keepers of family histories. The number of entries in these record albums bear witness to the persistence of the owner to enumerate all relatives in a permanent inventory. Those albums that survive today accomplish that purpose with an immediacy that is quite startling.

As the years progressed, when a relative passed on, the owner would return to her album and inscribe "deceased" or "death" near that loved one's hair, sometimes noting the date. These entries remained, heartfelt reminders of those who had passed away. In 1876 the author of the book *Ladies' Fancy Work* observed: "The hair of families thus preserved in a form not only pleasing and appropriate, but so lasting, as well . . . may be handed down from generation to generation as one of those 'heirlooms' always valued and sacred as a *memento mori* of those gone before."[2]

The custom of exchanging hair between friends was more widespread than the inclusion in books and albums. Locks of hair adorned letters or poems written to friends, either attached to the top of the page, or artlessly placed next to the signature at the bottom. Tiny individual tokens, only a couple of inches square, were also exchanged; just the lock of hair and a signature formed a cherished gift.

Memorial pieces made of hair proliferated from the most elaborate wreath with birds, butterflies, and flowers to the simple framed piece with just a lock of hair and the deceased's name. The larger the piece the more decoration it might include: a photograph of the deceased, beads, pearls, pieces of glass, or die-cut scrap.

When a piece was made after death, the hair was generally taken from the deceased during the preparations for burial. Keeping a lock of hair was the natural extension of the caring act, again the duty of the women in the family, of preparing the loved one's body for its travel, via the grave, to heaven. An author of a giftbook selection described the value of a hair memento:

Ay, a lock of hair is far better than any picture,—it is a part of the beloved object herself. . . .[3]

Collecting of hair from the living was a common practice. A commercially made porcelain "hair receiver," colorfully painted with flowers or butterflies, was a routine presence on the lady's boudoir dressing table. When a woman brushed her hair, she pulled single strands from her brush and deposited them in the receiver. The accumulated hair was used to make "rats" that filled the owner's buns and other fancy hair arrangements—and to make hairwork pieces.

The "silken strands," although difficult to work with,

This plait of hair which I place here ❧ As long As it may

A Lock of Hair

Few things in this weary world are so delightful as keepsakes. Nor do they ever, to my heart at least, nor to my eye, lose their tender, their powerful charm! How slight, how small, how tiny a memorial saves a beloved one from oblivion! . . .

Of all keepsakes, memorials, relics,—most dearly, most devotedly, do I love a little lock of hair; and oh, when the head it beautified has long mouldered in the dust, how spiritual seems the undying glossiness of the sad memento! All else gone to nothing, save and except that soft, smooth, burnished, and glorious fragment of the apparelling that once hung in clouds and sunshine over an angel's brow.

became the material for artistic invention, fashioned into many shapes and forms, from the simple plait and the triple-feather design called the "Prince of Wales Plumes" to elaborate roses and mated doves. Many sophisticated, professional-looking hairwork pieces were crafted purely as decorative objects to hang on parlor walls. Some were done by individuals, while others were shaped by groups of women, especially church societies, to commemorate their group or a passage of time. Finely crafted, these large and imposing pieces became more abstract—further from the hand or the heart. They lost the tender, personal aura of the little family or friendship albums. It is the simple, primitive documents that speak most clearly of the creator's emotions and feelings. The more unstudied and unpretentious they are, the louder their voice:

Some lasting memento my friends,
That shall tell me of days gone by,
Of friendships commenced, or grown strong as
     may be,
And respect, or affection, imply.

Though small the gift it speaks esteem,
Which years I hope will not impair,
A lock of hair though a trifle you deem
Is not without Our Father's care.

– LYDIA J. ENSIGN
Opening leaf of her hair book, 1840–1848
(Joe and Honey Freedman Collection)

should desire to preserve the treasure in some way that will testify our appreciation of its value, and when this can be done in a manner that is both pleasing to the taste and that will insure its prolonged or lasting preservation, it becomes a work which all may desire to be able to successfully practice. *The professional hair-manufacturers can doubtless perform this work more artistically, and bring it to a far higher degree of perfection than the mere amateur; but when we take into consideration the liability of having the hair of some other person substituted for that of our own cherished friend, or that careless hands have idly drawn through their fingers the tresses which it appears*

Stay ❧ *Will be a remembrance when I am far away.*

By the mid-19th century, when the hairwork rage was reaching its peak, publishers and the press observed the phenomenon and wrote to their audience. *The Jeweler's Book of Hairwork* was published in 1840 in London. In 1859 *Godey's Lady's Book* presented instructions for making hairwork pieces, and in 1864 *Peterson's Magazine* jumped on the bandwagon.[4] Most of the ladies' fancywork manuals gave instructions for making simple to elaborate pieces.

In 1876 Mrs. C. S. Jones, in her manual on ladies' fancywork, described the sentiment behind the art of hairwork:

✳ *As the hair is the only part of our beloved friends which can be kept in memoriam, it is natural that we*

almost sacrilegious to have even looked upon with a cold glance, the thought is repugnant. The ability to so arrange and secure each strand of the sacred treasure, becomes an accomplishment truly valuable, and worthy all the patience and skill required in its performance."[5]

The hairwork fad waned as the end of the century approached. The emotional and political climate of America was changing, and the practice of creating these mementos was deemed morbid, sentimental, and old-fashioned. Along with friendship albums, hairwork pieces were relegated to trunks in attics. Conditions destroyed some of the pages, paint and ink faded; but many of the plaits and coils remain exactly as they were the day they were made, a testament to love among family and friends.

CYNTHIA CAPRON BEGAN her handmade hair book (opposite) on May 15, 1842 at Halfmoon, Saratogo Co. New York. Bound in cardboard covered in brown and blue silk, it is stitched by hand and tied together with green silk ribbons. Cynthia's own hair is the first piece, followed by the other women in the family. Inside, the first leaf is inscribed, "Cynthia F. Caprons Hair book to be filled with locks of hair; as tokens of friendship long to be remembered." *(1842-1847, American; 5⅝ × 6½"; Joe and Honey Freedman Collection)*

IN THE HAIRWORK PIECE above, two sisters' (or cousins') hair is joined together in a heart shape; their names and an identification of each one's hair, "Lucy A. Farnam's—Plain— Abby G. Farnam's—Braid," encircle the piece. *(Lydia J. Ensign Hair Book, 1840-1848, American; 2½" diameter; Joe and Honey Freedman Collection)*

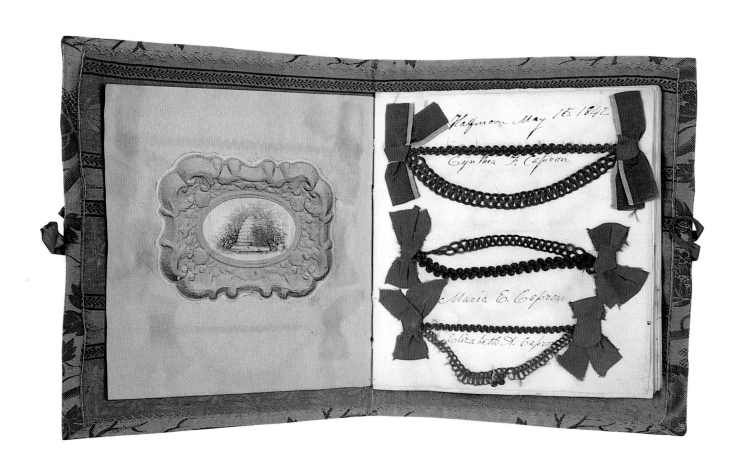

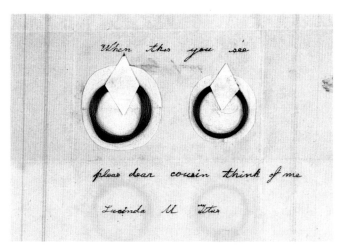

THE TINY, WALLPAPER-BOUND hair book (opposite, top) was made in Massachusetts and observes an engagement or marriage. *(American; 3¾ × 4¼"; Virginia Makis Collection)* The center token, probably from Pennsylvania, contains ringlets of hair from two cousins and folds like a letter. *(American; 6⅜ × 5⅝"; Joe and Honey Freedman Collection)* In 1852, in Antwerp, New York, Mary B. Clark paired the hair of a friend with a poignant memorial to a brother (opposite, bottom). *(American; 5 × 8")*

ON JANUARY 16, 1853, Mary Ann Brugh wrote in *Sarah Brough's* braid album (above): "Here is a bit of my / Heire my hand and / Heart, if I am gone / in a distant land. / If this you see you / Think of me for fear I / Might forgotten bee." *(1846-1853, American; Joe and Honey Freedman Collection)*

Exchange of Likenesses

o own the likeness of a loved one is a common heart's desire. But until the invention of photography, portraits—whether painted or sculpted—were costly, one-of-a-kind, and available only to the most affluent. Their successful creation could be accomplished only by skilled artists, each with an individual style. Thus, likenesses varied in the hands of different artists; they were "interpreted" rather than "true." ❡ Prior to photographs, the most popular and personal means of likeness exchange were portrait miniatures and, later, silhouettes—both diminutive, cherished images that could be held in the palm of one's hand, carried on a journey, or held to one's breast. ❡ From the first decades of the 1500s until the 1850s, portrait miniatures provided a fashionable means of owning a loved one's image. During the Renaissance, the dominance of religious art gradually shifted to acceptance of secular subject matter, fostering a tremendous growth in portraiture. The portrait miniature evolved in style and accuracy from the small-scale, meticulous renderings of illuminated manuscripts and in concept and shape from the European tradition of cast-metal or wax-portrait medallions. Their early name, "limning," derived from the word "illumination." The genre flourished on both sides of the Atlantic. ❡ Placed in elegant folding cases or set in fine jewelry, their presentation and intimate size reinforced the miniature's precious, delicate nature. Always treasured, they were often further personalized by the

inclusion of a setting on the reverse side in which to artfully display a woven lock of the subject's hair. Both men and women wore and carried images of their lovers, spouses, children, and ancestors. They exchanged them to celebrate engagements and to mark the passages of childhood. Some were painted posthumously as memorials. Queen Victoria wore a miniature of her beloved Albert in a bracelet from their early days together until her death, a span of 70 years. While the cost prohibited general exchange between friends, it did happen, particularly in royal circles, where a portrait miniature might be given as a friendship token or even as a reward for loyalty.

Miniatures were originally painted on vellum or parchment, but by the mid 1700s most were being executed on ivory, as it provided greater luminosity. The flesh in fine old miniatures still seems to glow from within. A painstaking process, it took as long to create as a full-sized oil painting, and it was fraught with technical problems. Ivory, while providing a background unparalleled in warmth and delicacy, was a difficult surface on which to work. Particularly when using watercolor, smudging could occur in an instant, with ruinous results. Cross-hatching or stippling compensated for or camouflaged these problems. Artists used sable brushes with as few as two or three hairs in order to attain the incredible detail in such a small scale.

The event of having a portrait miniature painted was a special one, and the clothes chosen for the sitting were the best finery owned—silks, lace, jewels. The result often provided accurate resemblances, and a deep insight into the subject's character and personality. In total, these images provide a document of the upper classes in their most sumptuous attire and graceful, if formal, postures.

In the late 18th and early 19th centuries in both Europe and America, silhouettes, and their opposite, hollow cuts, quickly became fashionable alternatives to portrait miniatures. Crafted with scissors and paper, they were cheaper and less time-consuming to make. Cut freehand or with the aid of a lamp to cast a shadow, the black form might be embellished with detail by pencil or paint, particularly gold, and then the completed image was glazed before being framed. Silhouettes were the first portrait medium available to the broad marketplace. With only the simplest of tools, many were crafted by women as a facet of decorative adornment for their homes.

Silhouettes were also made by professionals of varying talent, from the most sophisticated to the most primitive. Some of the itinerant "folk" artists in America, who developed strong, distinct traditions of portraiture as they traveled the small roads of this country, also offered the option of silhouette portraits. The majority of those that survive present the subject in exact profile, sometimes in embellished lace collars or bonnets. A more ambitious artist might

PHOTOGRAPHS provided a means for women to be recorded together. All the portraits pictured on pages 118-119 are daguerreotypes, except those in the accordion frame and the large group. The seven women, each with an anchor at her neck, were probably members of a society. (Harold Gaffin Collection) (Two women with fan, and two in white dresses: Collection of Roger and Kristine Williams) The portrait of two women (page 121) is an extraordinary example of a photographer's desire to document the warmth between two friends. Perhaps the one with the short hair had been ill, and the other was giving comfort. (Sixth-plate daguerreotype, circa 1851, American; Mona and Marc Klarman Collection. Photograph courtesy Mona and Marc Klarman) Before the birth of photography, small likenesses were rare and costly (opposite). The portrait miniature of the child is attributed to de Ten Eych of Albany, circa 1850. The hollow-cut of the woman, circa 1800, is stamped "Museum," one of Charles Willson Peale's marks. (Both: Roberta Hansen Collection) The silhouette of the young girl is embellished with pen and ink drawing, circa 1830. (Kelly and Jenner, American Antiques)

capture an entire family lined up in the suggestion of a domestic scene, complete with parlor table or pictures on the wall. Full-figured renderings were more difficult to accomplish and even more highly valued. Sometimes these family portraits were attached to a precreated background, painted or lithographed, of either an interior or a landscape with trees and gardens.

The term "silhouette" was derived from the name of Louis XV's Controller General of Finance, who initiated tax reforms in the 1750s that made him exceedingly unpopular. Etienne de Silhouette's name first became associated with things petty, small, or cheap. He practiced the hobby of cutting profiles out of paper, but it was one of his countrymen, Augustin Edouart, who in 1826 first called himself a "silhouettist."[1] As the medium of "shadow portraits" grew into vogue, they retained this initially disparaging name.

In a technique essentially the opposite of the silhouette, called "hollow cut," the profile was first drawn on white paper and then cut away. The resulting sheet was placed over either a second, black sheet or a piece of black silk. Many professionals, such as Charles Willson Peale and William Bache,[2] used small, portable machine-like devices that dramatically reduced the size of the sitter's outline to be in scale with paper size. But the purists held that the best hollow cuts were created by their expertise and a pair of scissors. William James Hubard, who established himself in New York in the 1820s, advertised that for 50 cents the sitter received "Correct Likeness in Bust cut by Master Hubard, Who, without the least aid from Drawing, Machine, or any kind of outline, but merely

THE TWO YOUNG WOMEN opposite wear identical bracelets, perhaps mourning jewelry, artfully displayed for the photograph. (Quarter-plate daguerreotype, circa 1852, American; Drew Heath Johnson Collection. Photograph courtesy Drew Heath Johnson)

by a glance at the Profile, and with a pair of common Scissors, instantly produces a Striking and Spirited Likeness;" all accomplished in twenty seconds.[3]

Women on both sides of the Atlantic became proficient at shadow portraiture, among them Princess Elizabeth, the daughter of George III; Mrs. Delany,[4] a well-born English woman later famous for her complex and highly correct cutwork flowers; and Nelly Custis, the granddaughter of George and Martha Washington. Many schoolgirls learned cut-paper designs as they were taught needlework and painting, and those who were proficient continued to execute designs in a variety of styles through their adult lives. A number became professionals, setting up shop in silhouette portraiture and spreading the craft beyond the exclusive circles of the well-to-do.

An artist's device for viewing subject matter in correct perspective and proportion, called the camera obscura (Latin for "dark chamber"), had been commonly used since the Renaissance, and historical references stretch back to the time of Aristotle. A closed, and thus darkened box, it had a glass lens at one end and a flat plane on the other. Light, reflected from the subject, traveled in a straight line through the lens and recorded the image on the opposite side, allowing the artist, looking through a small opening in the box, to copy or trace the image with felicity. Many experimenters, including Thomas Wedgewood, son of the great English potter, tried to make that image adhere to a substance, an emulsion. Some had succeeded in brief chemical reactions, but all efforts were fleeting and impermanent. William Henry Fox Talbot, an Englishman, pondered that elusive image and the desire to hold on to it in his now famous book, The Pencil of Nature. While on a trip to Italy in 1833, he used the camera obscura as he attempted to draw landscapes, and felt frustrated by his lack of skill:

And this led me to reflect on the inimitable beauty of the pictures of nature's painting which the glass lens of the camera throws upon the paper in its focus—fairy pictures, creations of a moment, and destined as rapidly to fade away.

It was during these thoughts that the idea occurred to me—how charming it would be if it were possible to cause these natural images to imprint themselves durably, and remain fixed upon the paper![5]

In France in 1839, Louis-Jacques-Mandé Daguerre, a painter well known for his dioramas, announced a photographic invention that would forever change the way people viewed the world. On January 7, at an event touted by the French government, Daguerre presented his image recorded on glass and his name became synonymous with the beginning of photography. His breakthrough set off reverberations around the civilized world. While many had experimented with "light drawing" or "light painting," none had been able to easily preserve the fleeting image. Politically, Daguerre was in the right place at the right time, and his government championed him to the exclusion of other inventors and their somewhat parallel contributions. The painter Paul Delaroche is said to have proclaimed, "From today, painting is dead!"

In 1827, a few years before Daguerre's spectacular pronouncement, Joseph-Nicéphore Niépce, a retired French military officer and scientist, had succeeded in stabilizing an image made by the camera. Termed "heliography," his photograph took eight hours to expose and his hand-applied emulsion was uneven and blotchy—neither a practical nor accessible process. Daguerre teamed up with Niépce for four years; when Niépce died, Daguerre went on to perfect the process himself. Through a still complicated chemical procedure, Daguerre "fixed," or made permanent, an image created by light rays hitting a copper sheet covered with silver compounds and then developed with mercury vapor.

The French government convinced Daguerre to accept a sum of 6,000 francs so that it could make the process freely available to the world, thus enhancing its country's reputation in the international scientific community. Daguerre agreed but, aware of international law, he quickly went to London to apply for copyright there. Granted it, he received royalties on his invention in England and, ultimately, was also awarded a pension from the French government. The French government's stamp of approval and subsequent promoting of Daguerre's process, combined with its great sharpness, helped rocket daguerreotypes to popular acceptance virtually overnight. Within a few years Daguerre's instruction manual for his procedures was translated into nine languages.[6]

Two sisters pose for a portrait (above) about the year 1843. *(Half-plate daguerreotype, American; 4 × 5"; Gary Ewer Collection. Photograph courtesy Gary Ewer)*

Meanwhile in England, William Henry Fox Talbot had been experimenting since his travels in 1833 with a different approach to fix an image recorded by rays of light. Talbot placed objects such as leaves or lace on paper that he had treated with alternate washes of salt and silver. Exposed to the light, the delicate, and very accurate, outlines of the object created a white silhouette on a darker ground. He was able to fix the image with a bath of alkaline iodide. Called "photogenic drawings," the images were made without use of a camera, similar to today's methods of contact printing or photograms. Building on earlier chemical discoveries by Sir John F. W. Herschel, Talbot continued his research to include the use of the camera, mostly home-devised boxes dubbed "little mousetraps" by his wife. Talbot invented the positive/negative system of making photographs, which he first called "Talbotypes" and later termed "calotypes."

Hearing of Daguerre's announcement, Talbot immediately made his own presentation at the British Royal Society on January 31, 1839, just three weeks later. Titled "Some Account of the Art of Photogenic Drawing—The Process by Which Natural Objects May Be Made to Delineate Themselves Without the Aid of the Artist's Pencil," Talbot presented a system of photography that offered multiples of an image, and he is generally thought of as the father of modern photography. Photography, with its amazing potential for recording directly from reality, was officially born.

Thus, two very distinctly different methods of capturing an image were developed and made public almost simultaneously in France and England. Both employed light-sensitive materials to make a permanent image, one on metal and the other on paper. The daguerreotype, a unique image, was very fragile and had to be cased under glass to survive. The calotype, with the potential for repeated printings, was by far the sturdier but in its early genesis both the negative and the positive were paper, and the resulting print was soft and fuzzy. Both required long exposures. While the daguerreotype had the potential for great sharpness, a portrait by the earliest photographers using that process took upwards of an hour to expose. The earliest photographic portraits appear staid and stiff as the sitter was often attached with clamps to hold the head rigid. However, rapid development in lens quality and the chemistry applied to the plate reduced the time to minutes and then mere seconds, and technique improved through constant experimentation and invention. Postures remained formal, but sitters began to truly give themselves to the camera.

 With the rise of photography, "writing with light," came a decline in the traditions of painted miniatures and unique-cut portraits. The new medium could quickly render its subject in hitherto-unknown clarity and detail, and rapid technical advances over its first 20 years allowed the production of multiple images from one negative. Photographic likenesses were accessible to everyone by the mid-19th century.

In England, as the quality of the calotype negative improved (making the positive much more crisp), some photographers followed the path blazed by Talbot. But Talbot

With the advent of photography women were finally able to exchange their likenesses (page 129). In late 1839, daguerreotypes were introduced in America to great enthusiasm and were followed by the less expensive, but still cased, ambrotype. The tintype, carte de visite, and cabinet cards were developed in rapid succession. Photographic albums were produced in a range of sizes, from tiny ones geared for tintypes to large and elaborately decorated celluloid versions designed for cabinet cards. (Celluloid albums: Barbara Rusch Collection)

To the Daguerreotype of an Estranged Friend

Still thou art mine, dear treasured gift,

Still art thou true to me,

Oh! blessed artist! naught can change

That kind look fixed by thee;

I gaze on lip, and cheek, and brow,

And almost fancy then is now.

– MARTHA CAMERON

Peterson's Ladies' National Magazine, 1854

was forceful about guarding his patents, and charged high yearly fees for the use of his invention. The daguerreotype was accessible to all who could afford the expensive equipment; particularly in America, where there were no patent restrictions to impede technical advancement, the public enthusiastically fell into a national love affair with the process. Edgar Allan Poe, effusing on the daguerreotype in the January 15, 1840 issue of *Alexander's Weekly Messenger*, wrote, "The instrument itself must be regarded as the most important, and perhaps the most extraordinary triumph of modern science."[7] He referred, as did many of his contemporaries, to "the most miraculous beauty"[8] of the process and continued, "The Daguerreotyped plate is . . . *infinitely* more accurate in its representation than any painting by human hands. If we examine a work of ordinary art, by means of a powerful microscope, all traces of resemblance to nature will disappear—but the closest scrutiny of the photogenic drawing discloses only a more absolute truth, a more perfect identity of aspect with the thing represented."[9]

The work of a number of the great American artisans is easily recognizable; Albert Sands Southworth and Josiah Hawes who partnered in a well-established studio in Boston; and the brothers William and Frederick Langenheim and Samuel Broadbent, all of Philadelphia. But most early photographers remain anonymous, as do many of their subjects. Some daguerreotypists were women, such as the artist who ran an advertisement in the Montreal *Transcript* of September 16, 1841:

> *Mrs. Fletcher,*
> *Professor and Teacher of the*
>
> **Photogenic Art**
>
> *Respectfully announces that she is prepared to execute Daguerreotype Miniatures in a style unsurpassed by any American or European artist.*

> *Those who have never enjoyed an opportunity of examining the Photogenic process, or a specimen of the art, cannot form an adequate idea of the extreme perfection, beauty, and wonderful minuteness of the*
>
> **Daguerrotype Pictures**
>
> *These are truly "the pencillings of nature," the production of minutes or seconds, and as perfect as the imagination can conceive. As the object looks at the moment it is taken, so is the representation. . . .*[10]

Lady Elizabeth Eastlake, an English writer on art and photography, observed in 1857 in *The London Quarterly Review* that in the fifteen years since "specimens of a new and mysterious art were first exhibited to our wondering gaze,"[11] photography was the most democratic media. While she could not accept that photography was art, it being too mechanical a process, she wrote:

> *For it is one of the pleasant characteristics of this pursuit that it unites men of the most diverse lives, habits, and stations, so that whoever enters its ranks finds himself in a kind of republic, where it needs apparently but to be a photographer to be a brother. The world was believed to have grown sober and matter-of-fact, but the light of photography has revealed an un-suspected source of enthusiasm.*[12]

On a more personal level, Elizabeth Barrett Browning expressed the public's enthusiasm for the new medium in a letter to her friend, Mary Russell Mitford, in 1843:

> *Do you know anything about that wonderful invention of the day, called the Daguerreotype? Think of a man sitting down in the sun and leaving his facsimile in all*

its full completion of outline and shadow, steadfast on a plate, at the end of a minute and a half? . . . It is not merely the likeness which is precious in such cases—but association and the sense of the nearness involved in the thing . . . the fact of the very shadow of the person lying there fixed for ever! It is the very sanctification of portraits.[13] . . . I would rather have such a memorial of one I dearly loved than the noblest artist's work ever produced.[14]

The faces, settings, styles, and postures captured in early daguerreotypes endure, providing a profoundly rich social document of a period. People were photographed together, particularly in immediate and extended families, and their relationships are revealed in expression and stance. And

added gold leaf to jewelry and pink cast to cheeks or to a rose; others subtly applied color to the subject's garment or background draperies. Former miniaturists were often hired to execute the painstaking color application process with the same skill and precision as when they worked on ivory. Later in the century, when photographs were produced on paper, colorists tinted or painted the entire image.

As in many arenas of scientific advancement, different inventors worked on perfecting the photographic process simultaneously, and approaches varied. In 1851 an Englishman, Frederick Scott Archer, followed Talbot's positive/negative innovation with the collodion wet plate. This process required the emulsion to be coated onto a glass plate just prior to exposure, and the negative to be processed immedi-

Grateful thanks you will receive ⚬ If your portrait here you leave.

repeatedly in this medium, women pose together. In these exquisite photographs, penetrating in detail, clarity, and depth, women stand with arms around each other's shoulders or waist, hands clasped or interlocked, or purposefully engaged in the intimate sweetness of sharing a book—all for the camera, all for the record. Whether it is a gesture of sister to sister or friend to friend, the bonds of affection are clear. While still an expensive medium of portraiture, some daguerreotypes were clearly exchanged by friends. Separation no longer meant relying on memory to see a loved one's face.

Many daguerreotypes were hand-colored, probably because the public was used to color in the painter's art and resisted a completely black and white image as not truly realistic. Sometimes praised but often castigated by purists, tinting was common practice. Some photographers simply

ately. A cumbersome method, it demanded a darkroom at hand; thus, if the photographer was out in the field, the darkroom had to travel with him. Extraordinary images were made in studios and on location around the world; pictures of tents and outfitted wagons depict the difficulties inherent in this process. The basic collodion method dominated the medium until the invention of dry plates by Richard Leach Maddox in 1871, which was introduced to the public in 1878.

An American, James Ambrose Cutting, produced another advance in 1854. While experimenting for a means to develop a negative system that would allow for multiple copies, Cutting actually developed a unique positive-appearing system, called "ambrotype" (from the Greek work "ambortos," meaning immortal or imperishable).[15] Seen against dark backgrounds, underexposed or bleached collodion negatives on glass appeared positive. Layered between glass plates, ambrotypes were finished with oval frames in the style of daguerreotypes. While lacking the delicacy and sparkle of daguerreotypes, they were considerably less expensive, selling for 10 cents apiece versus $1.00 to $5.00 for a daguerreotype.[16] Although daguerreotypers significantly reduced their prices, they could not be competitive. However, the ambrotype was not without its limitations, including its unique nature and Cutting's restrictive licensing demands, and it only claimed a ten-year period of popularity before it was obsolete.

In 1856, in a further development of the unique photograph called "tintype" or "ferrotype," sheets of blackened iron, rather than glass, were coated with an emulsion of collodion. Because of the low cost of the metal, this process was much more economical than glass-based photographs. In addition, the tintype was not fragile, and it did not need the bulky and expensive cases of daguerreotypes or ambrotypes. Tintypes remained widespread for decades, flourishing in little booths in fairgrounds as late as the 1920s—a lifespan of 80 years. And unlike the earlier processes, they were made on the spot, the metal plate coated, the photograph shot and processed. Often made with a multilens camera, multiple, if not identical, images were made, and if not instantaneous, at least very quickly; they could be placed in the hands of the consumer within six minutes.[17]

Just prior to the advent of the tintype, a negative printing process that was a further advancement of the collodion technique was patented in France by André Adolphe-Eugène Disdéri in 1854. The "carte de visite," or visiting card, was 2¼ by 3¾ inches in size. It offered for the first time the possibility of multiples of the same image, often made with a multilens camera, to just about anyone who wanted one. And millions did. A large studio on a bright day could book as many as 60 to 100 sittings and expect orders of a dozen photographs per client.[18] "Cartomania" had taken hold. In 1862, Oliver Wendell Holmes observed in *The Atlantic Monthly:*

Card portraits, as everybody knows, have become the social currency, the 'green-backs' of civilization. . . . The sitters who throng to the photographer's establishment are a curious study. They are of all ages, from the babe in arms to the cold wrinkled patriarchs and dames whose smiles have as many furrows as an ancient elm has rings that count it summers.

Attitudes, dresses, features, hands, feet betray the social grade of the candidates for portraiture. The picture tells us no lie about them. There is no use in their putting on airs; the make believe gentleman and lady cannot look like the genuine article. Ill-temper cannot hide itself under the simper of assumed amiability.[19]

Women, while few became as well known or successful as men, were a part of the profession since its inception, with several thousand practicing in the United States in the 19th century, particularly between 1860 and 1890.[20]

THIS UNUSUAL EARLY carte de visite (above), circa 1860s, depicts a small vignette of fourteen women in similar bonnets and capes, one holding the American flag. They wear tags, perhaps for identification, on their shoulders. (*Actual size*)

Another business idea, quick to be in vogue, was the sale of carte de visite images of the celebrated and famous. Images of Queen Victoria and her family were in great demand, and the Queen did her part to popularize the medium by avidly collecting photographs of her friends. Within a few years the size of the carte de visite was increased to 4 by 6 inches, and the slightly larger versions, frequently replete with painted studio backgrounds, columns topped with arrangements of greenery, and garden gates, were dubbed "cabinet cards."

Both the personal and celebrity portraits were collected in boxes and albums or printed small enough to fit in inexpensive jewelry settings. The first family album was patented in 1861 as a repository for collecting and organizing photographs, both tintypes and those printed on paper and pasted to cardboard. Albums ranged in size from the tiny 2-by-4-inch variety designed to hold tintype faces to oversize and elaborate versions bound in tooled leather, velvet, or celluloid, meant to match the family Bible in presentation. Some came attached to a stand that included a drawer for loose images. The array of status symbols on the parlor table was not complete without the photograph album.

(American tintype, circa 1880; 2 1/2 × 3 1/4")

New emulsions, camera sizes, and printing techniques further improved the photographic image over the last years of the century. The camera was no longer primarily the tool of professionals; it was finally placed in the hands of the common man. A picture could be taken on a whim, in an intimate setting, by anyone with the wish to record a loved one or friend.

Historically, portraiture had been a formal task—serious business that a sitter might commission only once in a lifetime, if at all. The length of a sitting, first for a painter, then a photographer, did not encourage a playful treatment. But with the introduction of inexpensive, quick photographic processes, people began to have fun. Photographed together, in irreverent poses, smiling, even laughing, a new spirit of friendliness and camaraderie entered the making of likenesses. Ordinary people could now give and receive an image of a dear one at very little cost. Many women who exchanged small tintypes or cartes de visite pasted them to the pages of friendship albums. Where she might have attached a lock of hair as a permanent memento, a woman could now attach her true likeness. Along with the words, "remember me," she could leave the gift of her face as well as her name.

$\mathcal{A}$ PAINTED BACKGROUND and its stand are visible in this unusual photograph (below) by Willis T. White, who probably intended to crop the edges in the final presentation. Rather than using the more common studio paraphernalia, these women chose dumbbells and lifted them in unison. *(Circa 1900, American; Images from the Past Collection)*

$\mathcal{P}$HOTOGRAPHS SUCH AS this amusing composition (opposite) were frequently made in the form of postcards to be sent to friends and relatives. *(American; 3½ × 5½")*

DECKER & WILBER,   CLEVELAND.

THREE WOMEN TOOK their rifles and fishing poles to the studio of Decker & Wilber in Cleveland, Ohio, for a group portrait (opposite). On the reverse side is penciled "Lady Hunters." *(Circa 1880s, American; 4¼ × 6½")*

FRIENDSHIP ALBUMS TYPICALLY held many photographs, pasted to pages in ones and twos. In an album marked 1861, Portland, Maine, each signed portrait measures only 1 × 1¼" (above). Its owner is identified only by the initials G. A. H. embossed on the cover. *(Barbara Rusch Collection)*

REMEMBER ME

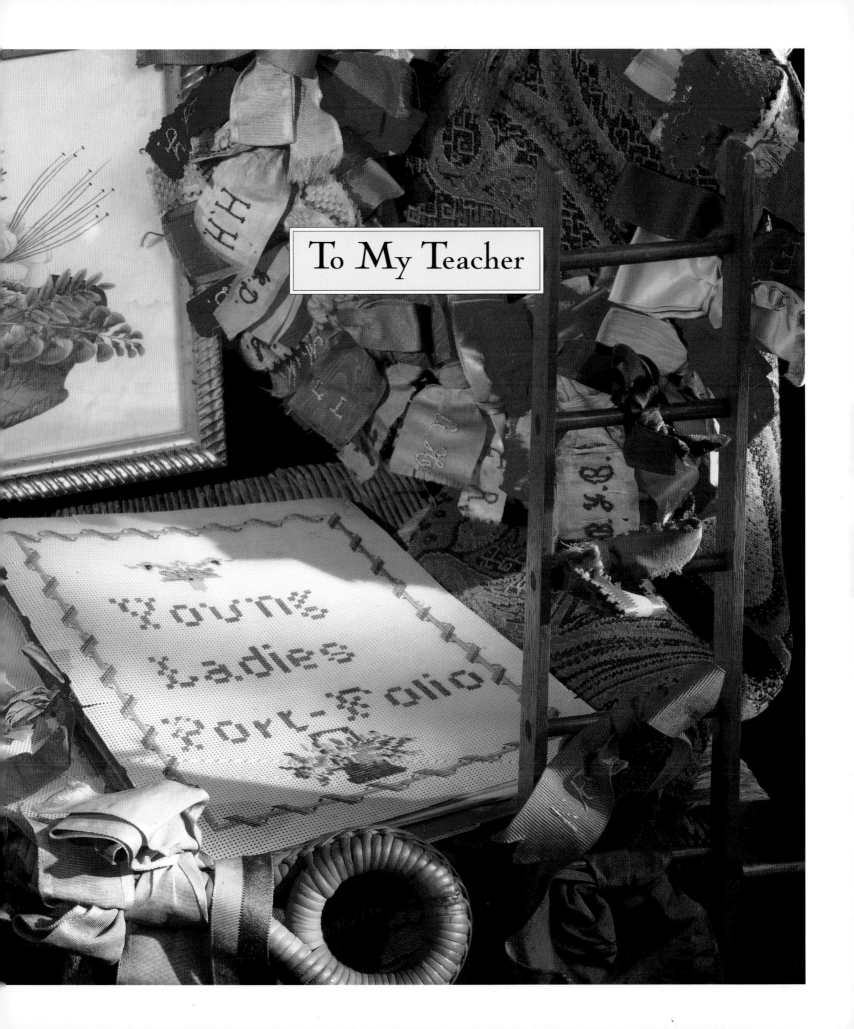

To My Teacher

entle passages and handmade tokens that celebrate the relationship between scholar and teacher can be found in old journals and among other personal documents of the 19th century. They are testaments to mutual respect, admiration, and friendship. In many small schools scattered around the country, both public and private, girls often learned from women not much older than themselves. These instructors in turn inspired many students to become teachers for a few years before they married. Other larger and long-established schools were led by strong, dedicated women who sought to impart knowledge and skills to young girls. Some of these teachers' names and influence are just beginning to come to light. ¶ On August 5, 1853, the school year came to an end at a female academy in Washington, Maine, a small town 20 miles southeast of Augusta. Washington was primarily an agricultural community with a number of sawmills boosting the economy. That morning, Miss Ethelda Coggin addressed a gathering of "venerable sires" and parents, and particularly her female "scholars." The day, as she recorded it, was a cool one. ¶ She was well prepared for the event, with a speech handwritten on pale blue paper. Miss Coggin referred to the past months and the weather changes, and then, with sadness, to the loss of one of their own— a father, a leader in the community, and a man clearly connected to the academy. In her address she tried to prepare her young charges for the eventual

THE FRAMED WATERCOLORS (preceding pages) are examples of schoolgirl art, both in style and content. *(Roberta Hansen Collection)* "The Literary Casket" and the "Young Ladies Portfolio" contain issues of a monthly handwritten paper produced from 1858 to 1860. In a charming American custom, friendship wreaths, ladders, and canes were assembled as group efforts by friends to celebrate important passages in young girls' lives. Often each ribbon was embroidered with the initials of the giver.

THIS FINE, EARLY EXAMPLE of schoolgirl art (above) was perhaps done as a self portrait. Inscribed over the girl's head is, "We met but once but friend- / ship gives / This simple boon to thee / If others scorn the life / I live / Think not unkind of me." Signed "Zenith," and rendered in pencil and watercolor, the piece dates to circa 1830. *(American; 6¾ × 6¼"; Nancy Rosin Collection)*

loss of loved ones and separations from friends and family. Ethelda Coggin read:

> *There are many pleasing associations connected with this antiquated building, for here have been formal ties of friendship which nothing but death can sever. At the close of our exercises in the school room teachers and scholars must seperate and probably never to meet again as we now are: some will go in one direction, and some in another: some to one occupation and some to another, but will not our thoughts often return to this old Academy? . . .*
>
> *Some of us may meet here again but not all, therefore I bid you all an affectionate farewell with the hope of meeting you in heaven where parting is never known.*[1]

Miss Coggin saved her speech, and, with it, the handwritten tokens that each young pupil presented as a final gift "To my Teacher." On 28 small sheets of paper, mostly pale blue like their teacher's, the girls wrote or copied friendship poems of the period. They attached silk ribbons (woven through double slits in the paper) and further enhanced some with braided wreaths or locks of hair. The girls probably brought the ribbons from home, as sisters' ribbons are of the same pattern. The little girls, whose penmanship was not as fine as that of the older ones, copied poems from their elders.

In colonial times education began for most children in the dame schools, small community schools run by women generally in their own homes. Both boys and girls attended, sometimes as early as age two or three, allowing their mothers time to run their households. This manner of education, and the affection generated between dame and child, continued well into the 19th century. In her mem-oirs, Lucy Larcom wrote of her early education in the 1820s, "I learned my letters in a few days, standing at Aunt Hannah's knee while she pointed them out in the spelling-book with a pin, skipping over the 'a b abs' into words of one and two syllables, thence taking a flying leap into the New Testament, in which there is concurrent family testimony that I was reading at the age of two years and a half. Certain it is that a few passages in the Bible, whenever I read them now, do not fail to bring before me a vision of Aunt Hannah's somewhat sternly smiling lips, with her spectacles just above them, far down on her nose, encouraging me to pronounce the hard words."[2]

Reading was taught initially from a hornbook (a flat piece of wood with a handle, to which was attached a piece of paper bearing the alphabet and a religious piece such as the Lord's Prayer) and later from *The New England Primer*, spelling books, the Bible, and the catechism. The dames also provided training in deportment and instruction in arithmetic.

For the girls, the most important concentration was on the rudiments of sewing. The needle was so precious that a little girl usually had only one, which she brought to and from school each day, sometimes facing punishment if she forgot it. In some cases, needles and thimbles were passed out at the beginning of the work session and collected at the end of the day. Girls as young as four or five began with a sampler, traditionally called an "exampler," or a "pattern book" of stitches.

Current research reveals that most antique samplers and needlework pictures were made by young women in school, under the instruction of schoolmistresses, rather than at home. Although these teachers remain anonymous, they were very accomplished needlewomen who created whole "schools" of style, drawing particular band patterns, repeating floral or decorative motifs, favoring certain types of stitches and verses. Because the girls who studied under a fine teacher often went on to become teachers themselves, the distinctive patterns of an early instructor developed into regional styles, passed on from generation to generation.

The simplest form of sampler, drawn by a teacher on a piece of canvas, linen, or muslin, was used to teach the alphabet and the practical skill of labeling household linens with initials and numbers. Thus, many of the most rudimentary samplers contain the alphabet and numerals from at least 1 to 10. Early stitching lessons were also executed on darning samplers, illustrating a range of practical sewing skills on one piece of linen.

As girls went on to higher levels of schooling at finishing schools or academies, their workmanship advanced, and they produced art on linen or "lindsey-woolsey" (a combination of linen and wool) in silk threads. Whole worlds of descriptive imagery leapt from their needles. Perspective was inconsequential; many different varieties of fruit and flowers grew on one vine, and animals and people cavorted together in unlikely scenes and sizes. The finest pieces were hung on parlor walls like diplomas, testimonies to the completion of the young women's education.

Some samplers were pastoral pictures or town scenes, some depicted a girl's own house, and others were family genealogies or mourning pictures. In this manner, family names, histories, and homes became documents; the young needlewomen, under the guidance of their instructresses, were recording their history for themselves and posterity.

While it is rare for a teacher's name or initials to be included in a piece, even though she created the design, the girl who stitched it almost always signed her full name and gave her age and the date. The samplers' distinctive regional and stylistic designs have enabled some unsung teachers to become identified by name: Mrs. Sarah Fiske Stivours of Salem, Massachusetts, who taught for at least 20 years[3]; Miss Mary Balch of Providence, whose career spanned 45 years[4]; and Miss Sarah Pierce of Litchfield, Connecticut, who instructed for 40 years.[5]

The verses chosen for samplers covered subjects as varied as virtue, piety, patriotism, praise of learning, love and marriage, family, nature, industry, religion, sorrow— and friendship, as in these two examples:

Friendship's a pure a Heav'n descended flame
Worthy the happy region whence it came
The sacred eye that virtuous spirits binds
The golden chain that links immortal minds

(1807)[6]

(Alfred P. Malpa Collection)

To my Teacher Ethelda Coggan

Remember me when gone away

And I the same will do

And when you're with your friends at home

then I'll remember you

Forget me ah forget me not

When evenings shades decend

For then my thoughts still turn to thee

My fondly cherished friend.

August 4th. 1853

From your pupil

– ANGELINE HILTON

(Alfred P. Malpa Collection)

*E*THELDA COGGIN'S LECTURE on the final day of school is placed on a small desk surrounded by her pupils' farewell tokens (page 146). Each includes a poem of friendship and a lock of hair tied with a ribbon. Typical to the teacher and scholar exchanges were Rewards of Merit and giftbooks such as "The Teacher's Gift or Instructive Stories for Children and Youth," by "a Lady" (1854). The friendship cane is tied with many different colored ribbons. *(Ethelda Coggin papers: Alfred P. Malpa Collection)*

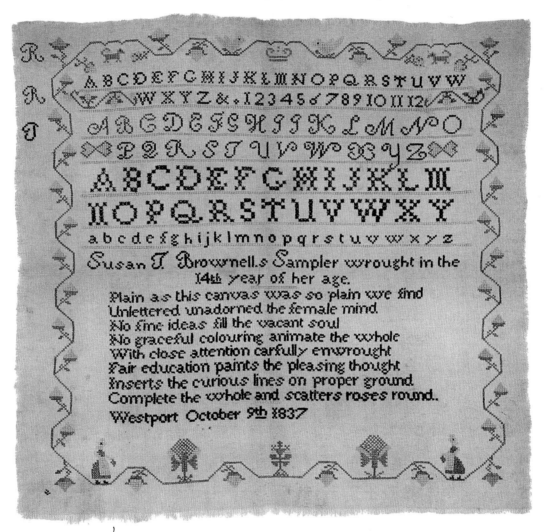

*Y*OUNG SUSAN J. BROWNELL practiced her test stitches outside the border of her simple sampler (above) intending that they would be covered by a frame. The poignant verse describes the period's attitude toward female education. *(1837, American; 14¾ × 13¾"; Mary Donaldson and Robert Batt, M. D. Collection)* When Susanna Bell stitched her band sampler (opposite) in the "11th year of her age 1813," she featured a classic verse. *(Silk on linen; American; 16 × 10¾"; Robin Fake Collection; photograph courtesy M. Finkel & Daughter)*

A solitary blessing few can find
Our joys with those we love are intertwined
And he whose wakeful tenderness removes
The obstructing thorn which wounds the friend he loves
Smooths not anothers rugged path alone
But scatters roses to adorn his own.

(1813)[7]

Generally, upon completion of some local education, daughters of more affluent parents were sent to boarding schools to be "finished." There they studied arithmetic, geometry, geography, ciphering, French, history, dancing, music and painting, and needlework. While some lived with aunts or other relatives, others boarded with women who, out of financial need, acted as teachers themselves. Their mission was respected; it was a calling. In 1771, Anna Green Winslow was in her twelfth year, a schoolgirl in Boston far from her home in Nova Scotia. Entries in her journal indicate that her education was being carefully monitored according to the standards of the day by her aunt, with whom she resided:

> *I have spun 30 knots of linning yarn, and (partly) new footed a pair of stockings for Lucinda, read a part of the pilgrim's progress, coppied part of my text journal (that if I live a few years longer, I may be able to understand it, for aunt sais, that to her, the contents as I first mark'd them, were an impenatrable secret) play'd some, tuck'd a great deal (Aunt Deming says it is very true) laugh'd enough, & I tell aunt it is all human nature if not human reason. And now, I wish my honored mamma a very good night.[8]*

Many of these schoolgirls became especially accomplished at drawing and painting. Besides conventional watercolor and oil painting, they learned a popular style of painting, often inserted in copybooks and albums, called theorem, Poonah, or Oriental painting. A method of stenciling, theorem painting involved preparing a separate horn paper, or "theorem," for each color in the work. Open spaces in the theorems were painted with a bristle brush, held upright and manipulated quickly in a circular motion. Moving the paint from the center toward the edge of the shape caused the edge to pick up more color and appear as a slight halo.[9] Subject matter was generally fruit and flower baskets or birds and butterflies.

Fine handwriting, an attribute prized in England, was another important feature of an American girl's education. Some girls, such as Anna Green Winslow, attended special schools for writing. "My aunt Deming says, it

FOR THIS PORTRAIT of ten schoolgirls with their teacher the photographer used Rembrandt style of lighting, placing the lights high from the right side. As the exposure needed to be several seconds in length, the sharpness of the subjects' faces is remarkable. The cheeks of each girl have been lightly tinted pink in this half-plate daguerreotype, circa 1844. *(American, 4¼" × 5½", Dennis A. Waters Collection; photograph courtesy Dennis A. Waters)*

is a grief to her, that I don't always write as well as I can, *I can write pretily.*"[10] Carefully forming their letters, the girls filled copy books with poetry and lessons. By the mid-19th century, a fancy Spencerian script and other calligraphic squiggles and flourishes were taught in the schools.

The length of a boarding-school education varied from a few months to several years. Whatever the span, the girls developed warm friendships with each other and, as their schoolgirl albums bear witness, with their teachers as well. Eliza Southgate, born in Scarborough, Maine, in 1783, attended boarding school in Medford, Massachusetts. In a letter home, she wrote of her new teacher:

Boston, February 13, 1798

Hon. Father:

I am again placed at school under the tuition of an amiable lady, so mild, so good, no one can help loving her; she treats all her scholars with such a tenderness as would win the affection of the most savage brute, tho' scarcely able to receive an impression of the kind. I learn Embroidery and Geography at present and wish your permission to learn Musick.

–ELIZA SOUTHGATE[11]

*I*n more than one album begun at an academy or boarding school there is evidence that the owner later became a teacher herself and received messages of gratitude and friendship from her own students. Caroline E. Mellish started her album as a schoolgirl and carried it with her throughout her teaching days. From 1856 to 1861 her scholars made entries. At Stoneville School in Auburn, Massachusetts, Jennie Mayer wrote:

To My Teacher

I see thee still—though far away,
From my young vision new,
I gaze upon thine eyes sweet ray,
Thy fair and lofty brow.

I hear thy voice of melting power
Those tones of holy thrill;
In fancies of the midnight hour,
I dream I see thee still.

–JENNIE E. MAYER
FEBRUARY 12TH, 1861, AUBURN, MASS
Caroline E. Mellish Album, 1851-1878

*I*n 1839, when Armida (Maria) Pinkham set off to attend Monmouth Academy, she carried an album dedicated to her by her father. Over the next eight years she filled it with entries by her friends, and by her own students as she, too, became a teacher at the Academy. One of Armida's own teachers wrote, "I will only direct your attention to the importance of cultivating a grateful remembrance of those who have been your instructors." And a late entry, whether inscribed by teacher or scholar, speaks of the importance of the album as a record of those relationships:

To Miss Maria

May the perusal of this Album which is intended as a repository of friendships offering whose silent eloquence more rich than words, tells of the writers faith. Be a source from which in after years may arise many pleasant recollections of by gone days. May friendship's hand be ever extended to you by all who on these sacred pages are permitted to engrave thier memory. And may recollections of by gone days

like the mellow ray of a departing sun fall sadly yet
tenderly on your mind. And age be like an autum
day. That glides in tranquil peace away.

– ELIZABETH J. BROWN
MONMOUTH, JUNE 4, 1845
Armida M. Pinkham Album, 1839-1847
(Helen Walvoord Collection)

*A*nother young woman, Harriet Rider from Grafton, Connecticut, taught school in Stukely, Lower Canada, during 1840 and 1841. As spring broke, probably just before her return home, she went out into nature and composed with exuberance in her album:

> *The world is full of Poetry—the air*
> *Is living with its spirit; and the waves*

– CHASTINA BOWKER, STUKELY
MAY 1841
Harriet Rider Album, 1835-1846
(Nancy Rosin Collection)

*L*ucy Larcom of Lowell, Massachusetts, wrote an account of her years as a mill "operative" when she was 12 or 13. In it she described her desire for education that persisted throughout 13-hour days in the various duties she assumed in her 10 years in the mills. She managed to take courses in the evenings and designed for herself an educational program of reading classics and other contemporary literature. Lucy and her friends were fortunate that Lucy's older sister Emilie "care[d] more to watch the natural development of our minds than to make us follow the direction of hers. She was really our teacher, although she never assumed that

Let us be friends, in tender years ∾ *When infant genius first appears.*

> *Dance to the music of its melodies,*
> *And sparkle in its brightness.*[12]

*H*er spirit must have been infectious, as her two nieces, Sarah and Chastina Bowker, who were also her students, wrote of her upcoming departure with sadness and great affection. That precious album traveled to and from Harriet's year up north:

> *My ever dear Aunt one happy year has past in*
> *which I have attended your school and have enjoyed*
> *inexpressible pleasure in receiving your instruction and*
> *shall ever feel grateful for your kindness to me. But*
> *now, dear aunt, we are called to part and will you*
> *accept this small tribute of love and affection from*
> *your niece.*

position. Certainly I learned more from her about my own capabilities, and how I might put them to use, than I could have done at any school we knew of, had it been possible for me to attend one. I think she was determined that we should not be mentally defrauded by the circumstances which had made it necessary for us to begin so early to win our daily bread."[13]

Emilie formed her group of girls into "a little society for writing and discussion, to meet fortnightly . . . [we] named ourselves 'The Improvement Circle'."[14] These young, intelligent women initiated two newspapers while working in the mills of Lowell. Contributors to these handwritten papers later wrote for *The Lowell Offering*.

There are other samples of coteries of young women, probably guided by an older girl or a teacher, producing

*A*RMIDA M. PINKHAM *treasured the relationships she experienced with her scholars. O*ver the years many young girls wrote in her album; this is Martha A. Dexter's page. *(1839-1847, American; Helen Walvoord Collection)*

To My Teacher

"Shall I forget thee? When the vernal rose
In early spring, no longer buds or blows,
When birds of sweetest notes forget to sing,
And blooming flowers no longer deck the spring,
When through the vale the stream shall cease to flow;
Then! not till then! shall I forget thee! No!"

Martha A Dexter

Wayne April 20th 1845

*T*HROUGHOUT THE SCHOOL YEAR *teachers presented* Rewards of Merit *to deserving scholars for all manner of exemplary works. Thousands have survived, from the early hand-drawn and painted ones to the printed and hand-colored examples or chromolithographed counterparts. M*ore the exception than the rule, women are pictured as the teachers, the nurturers, in these three mid-19th-century rewards *(opposite), each measuring* 5¾ × 3". *(Lower reward: 1849; Nancy Rosin Collection)*

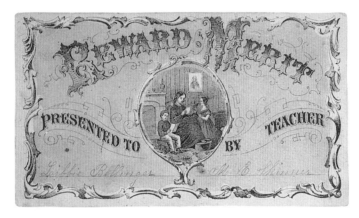

handwritten papers. In October 1858 in Newburgh, New York, two papers were started: *The Literary Casket* and *The Young Ladies Portfolio*. Each was produced monthly, coming out on alternate fortnights. A determination to succeed runs through all of their issues. The editors of *The Young Ladies Portfolio* declared in their first issue, "We do not intend to allow the word *fail* to be *mentioned* in our hearing, and we most assuredly shall not permit our columns to exhibit any practical evidence of the existence of such a word in the language."[15]

Both papers, produced on lined paper and hand-tied together, follow much of the format described by Lucy Larcom. All the issues, averaging 34 pages in length, are handwritten, each in a single hand. Although that hand varies from issue to issue, it is difficult to imagine that many copies of each could have been made. Each begins with an editorial and continues with articles on such subjects as "Avarice," "Health," "The Pleasures of Memory," "Industry and Indolence," "Knowledge is Power," and stories of specific events and adventures, like "My First Visit to New York," and "Riding Down the Hill on a Shovel." Included, too, are some letters from women friends and relatives, particularly aunts, and each issue is closed confidently with "questions, puzzles, enigmas" to be answered in the following issue. The surviving issues are preserved within handmade folios with covers sewn by hand and lined in silk, each embroidered with the title and a decorative border of flowers on punchpaper.

Whatever the nature and depth of education, from the modest dame schools to academies, seminaries, and boarding schools, young women sought learning, and in the process the relationships between teacher and scholar were cemented in special ways. Inspired by their instructresses, many of those scholars passed on the gift of knowledge that older women had offered to them. "When I thought what I should best like to do, my first dream—almost a baby's dream—about it was that it would be a fine thing to be a school teacher, like Aunt Hannah."[16]

After leaving the mills of Lowell in the 1840s, Lucy Larcom, herself then a teacher in Mississippi, finally achieved her dream education:

> *Only a mile or two away from this pretty retreat [the school at which she taught] there was an edifice towards which I often looked with longing. It was a seminary for young women, probably at that time one of the best in the country, certainly second to none in the West. . . . The stately limestone edifice, standing in the midst of an original growth of forest-trees, two or three miles from the Mississippi River, became my home—my student home—for three years. The benefits of those three years I have been reaping ever since, I trust not altogether selfishly. It was always my desire and my ambition as a teacher to help my pupils as my teachers had helped me. . . .*
>
> *The great advantage of a seminary course to me was that under my broad-minded Principal I learned what education really is: the penetrating deeper and rising higher into life, as well as making continually wider explorations; the rounding of the whole human being out of its nebulous elements into form, as planets and suns are rounded, until they give out safe and steady light. This makes the process an infinite one, not possible to be completed at any school.*
>
> *Returning from the West immediately after my graduation, I was for ten years or so a teacher of young girls in seminaries much like my own Alma Mater. The best result to me of that experience has been the friendship of my pupils,—a happiness which must last as long as life itself.*[17]

*T*HIS CLASS PORTRAIT (above), probably from a small
female academy, was perhaps taken at the end of the school year.
An American half-plate daguerreotype, circa 1843, it measures
4 ¼ × 5 ½″. *(Gary Ewer Collection; photograph courtesy Gary Ewer)*

LOVE AND THE FLOWERS.

Language of Flowers.

Basket ↓

Hidden Languages

THE LANGUAGE OF FLOWERS
BOQUET
THE
FLORAL
ALBUM
J.C.RIKER
FLOWERS OF
FLORAL
AUTOGRAPH ALBUM.
LOVELINESS

On the title page of *The Floral Album*, a woman in a Grecian gown sits beside an album open to reveal flowers sketched on a page. The woman, arms outstretched, is receiving a spray of Flora's bounty from a cherub. In Frances S. Osgood's *The Poetry of Flowers*, the title, wrapped around a delicate urn, is in turn encircled by a garland of flowers. Each blossom in these images bears a message; for example, the primrose means "have confidence in me," and the pansy signifies tender and pleasant thoughts. ¶ Historically, while lovers and friends often proclaimed their feelings in poetic form, they also believed that objects from flowers to gems held hidden significance. The choice of a token could convey the depth of their feeling, often more eloquently than words. ¶ Robert Tyas in his 1869 edition of *Language of Flowers* introduced the subject: "Before the different languages which are now common among men were developed, various animate and inanimate objects were made use of instead of words for the purpose of giving expression to thoughts. Animals, birds, and flowers were emblems of individuals and their characteristics; and though sometimes erroneously assigned, they are yet very generally adopted. . . . It is asserted that the Chinese possess an alphabet made up of figures of plants and roots. The rocks of Egypt are marked with representations of vegetables foreign to that country, which tell us of the conquests achieved by its ancient inhabitants."[1] ¶ Tradition and

FRIENDSHIP ALBUMS and sketchbooks were often titled by
the publisher with names of flowers or bouquets. Within the pages
of these books women gave each other the gift of flowers, often
for the significance of their inherent message (preceding pages).
*(Theorem rose: Jane Eugenia Baily Album, Montreal, 1836, Barbara
Rusch Collection; morning glory: 1831, Helen Walvoord Collection)*

THE HAND-COLORED LITHOGRAPH (above), entitled
the "Rose of Allandale," served as the sheet music cover of a
popular ballad written by Charles Jefferys, and was published in
New York, circa 1840. *(6¾ × 7¾")*

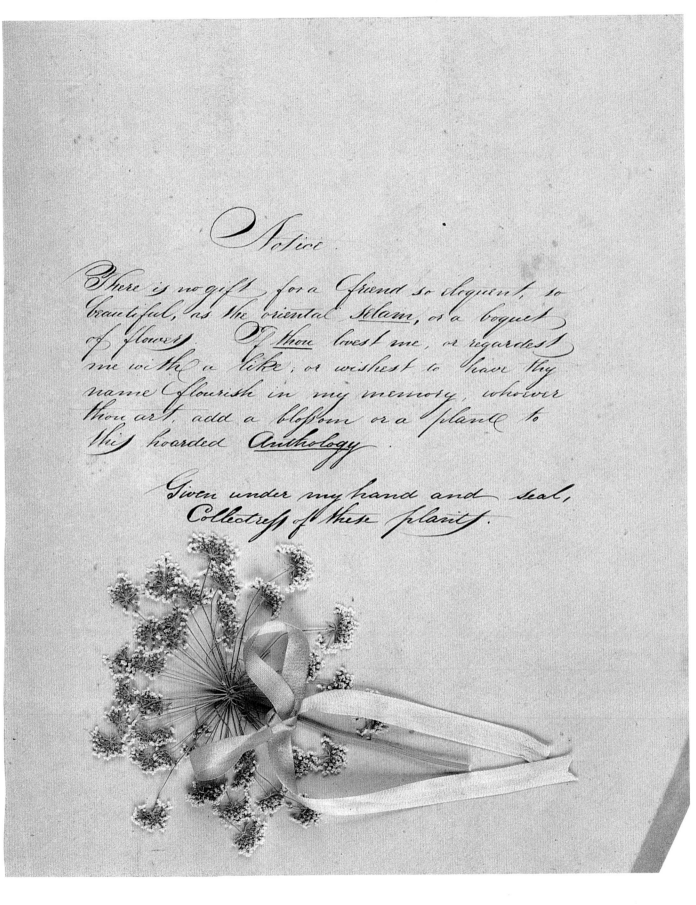

Notice.

There is no gift, for a Friend so eloquent, so beautiful, as the oriental Selam, or a boquet of flowers. If thou lovest me, or regardest me with a like, or wishest to have thy name flourish in my memory, whoever thou art, add a blossom or a plant to this hoarded Anthology.

Given under my hand and seal, Collectress of these plants.

recorded source material differ on which meanings were applied to certain objects, interpretations that evolved over centuries. Yet many symbols have retained their significance over long periods of time. Meaning also depended on the specific use of a symbol. If a flower, such as a rose, was given out of affection it meant love; if its image appeared on a memorial piece, it conveyed sorrow. Whether communicated through a watercolor of a wreath of ivy (friendship) on the page of a friendship album, or a brooch depicting clasped hands (in trust forever), an emotional bond was strengthened by a symbolic gift:

> —A flower I love
> Not for itself,
> but that its name is linked
> With names I love.
> —A talisman of hope
> And memory.[2]

The custom of these exchanges, often in combination with poetry, stems from ancient times. Egyptian hieroglyphics and Greek and Roman mythology included the symbolism, even the deificaton, of flowers. The Bible, too, contains many references to symbols in nature as well as the medicinal value of plants and herbs. Through many centuries a major source for understanding the symbolism of plants was the herbal, a book of descriptions of plants compiled for medical purposes.

Selam, the oriental language of flowers, a Persian poetical art, was brought to Europe by Charles II of Sweden, who spent five years in exile in Turkey after being defeated

in 1709 by Peter the Great. Charmed by its expressive and mysterious vocabulary, Charles' courtiers adopted the language as one of the heart, and it spread from court to court (with many alterations in the Persian meanings) throughout the western world.[3]

In 1838 in Huntington, Connecticut, Rebecca Beach Judson acknowledged the origin of the symbolic tradition in her herbarium: "There is no gift for a friend so eloquent, so beautiful, as the oriental *selam* or a bouquet of flowers." Other women echoed the sentiment, frequently including the following lines from James G. Percival's poem in their albums:

> In Eastern Lands, they talk in flowers,
> And they tell in a garland their loves and cares;
> Each blossom that blooms, in their garden bowers,
> On its leaves a mystic language bears:
> Then gather a wreath from the garden bowers,
> And tell the wish of thy heart in flowers.[4]

One of the earliest surviving English-language messages that incorporated objects to create a poetic meaning was written by Lady Mary Wortley Montagu on March 16, 1717, during a sojourn in Turkey. Lady Mary and her husband, the newly appointed ambassador to Turkey, were living in Constantinople. As her great grandson, Lord Wharncliffe, wrote in the introduction to her edited letters, "Lady Mary amused herself, and delighted her friends by a regular correspondence."[5] Many of these letters were directed to her sister, the Countess of Mar, Lady Rich:

To the Lady Rich

I have got for you, as you desire, a Turkish love-letter, which I have put into a little box, and ordered the

REBECCA BEACH JUDSON'S herbarium proffered an enticing invitation (opposite) to contribute to her anthology. (1840, American; 5½ × 3¾"; Robert Fraker Collection)

captain of the *Smyrniote* to deliver it to you with this letter. The translation of it is literally as follows: The first piece you should pull out of the purse is a little pearl, . . . and must be understood in this manner:

Pearl	Fairest of the young.
Clove	You are as slender as the clove!
	You are an unblown rose!
	I have long loved you, and you have not known it!
Jonquil	Have pity on my passion!
Paper	I faint every hour!
Pear	Give me some hope.
Soap	I am sick with love.
Coal	May I die, and all my years be yours!
A rose	May you be pleased, and your sorrows mine!
A Straw	Suffer me to be your slave.
Cloth	Your price is not to be found.
Cinnamon	But my fortune is yours.
A match	I burn, I burn! My flame consumes me!
Gold thread	Don't turn away your face from me.
Hair	Crown of my head!
Grape	My two eyes!
Gold wire	I die—come quickly.
And by way of postscript:	
Pepper	Send me an answer.

You see this letter is all in verse, and I can assure you there is as much fancy shown in the choice of them, as in the most studied expressions of our letters; there being, I believe a million of verses designed for this use. There is no colour, no flower, no weed, no fruit, herb, pebble, or feather, that has not a verse belonging to it; and you may quarrel, reproach or send letters of passion, friendship, or civility, or even of news, without ever inking your fingers.[6]

*T*he late-18th century Romantic movement was also influential in popularizing plant symbolism. Poets, writers, and painters were inspired to lose themselves in nature, to be at one with it, to worship it, and to glorify it in their writings. Nature was morality; Rousseau wrote, "I feel therefore I am." But for the less educated, newly affluent middle class, Romanticism was diluted into sentimentalizing the movement's ideals. And, too, rather than espousing a philosophy, nature provided a way to make life more charming, amusing, and romantic with a small "r."

In addition, the study of botany, part of the schoolgirl's curriculum, was viewed as particularly appropriate for women, as expressed by Mrs. Almira H. Lincoln, a vice principal of Troy Female Seminary:

> *The study of Botany seems peculiarly adapted to females; the objects of its investigation are beautiful and delicate; its pursuits, leading to exercise in the open air, are conducive to health and cheerfulness. It is not a sedentary study which can be acquired in the library, but the objects of the science are scattered over the surface of the earth, along the banks of the winding brooks, on the borders of precipices, the sides of mountains, and the depths of the forest.[7]*

*T*he study of "elegant" botany was not intended to end in the classroom, but was meant to lead to the pleasure and knowledge of "floriculture." Most middle-class women lovingly tended a garden, ornamental rather than utilitarian, on some scale. The populace became passionate about flowers, on their own grounds and in the great public gardens and conservatories that were established in the

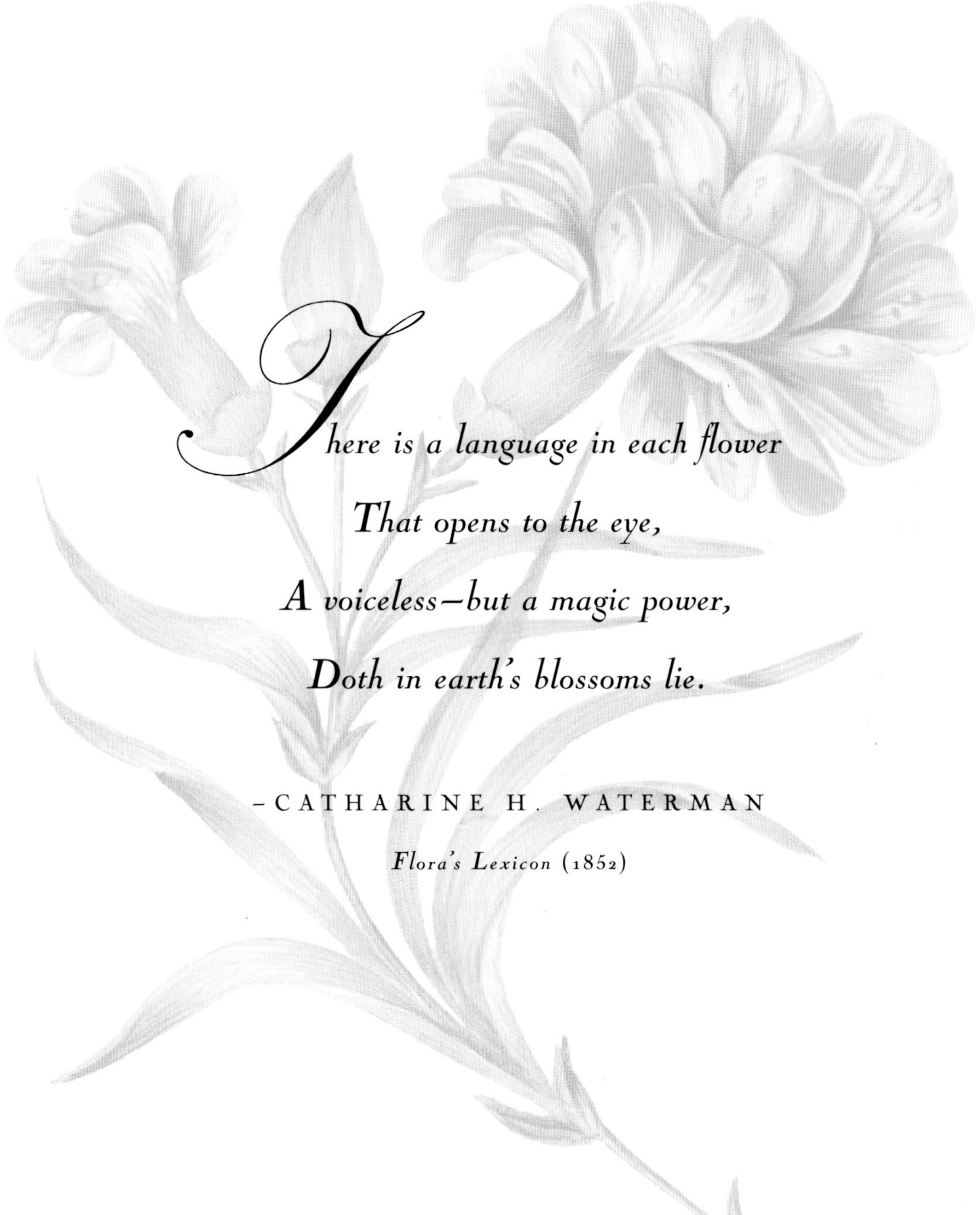

There is a language in each flower

That opens to the eye,

A voiceless—but a magic power,

Doth in earth's blossoms lie.

—CATHARINE H. WATERMAN

Flora's Lexicon (1852)

19th century. Exotic plants were gathered from around the world, and the public flocked to view them. Ladies wore flowers, carried them in small, round bouquets or nosegays called "tussie mussies," and decorated their homes with them. People enjoyed them not only for their beauty and scent, but for their meanings. Initially, books on botany and floriculture had included references to floral symbolism, but as the rage of using flowers as a language caught on, floral dictionaries became successful in themselves, and many versions were published in England, France, and America. A mid-19th century pamphlet titled *A Correct Dictionary of Flowers*, small enough to be tucked into a purse for repeated reference, opens with "Flowers are the Alphabet of Angels, whereby they write on hills and fields mysterious truths."[8] *Durch die Blume*

teen editions), "Flowers have also been symbols of the affections probably ever since our first parents tended theirs in the garden of God's own planting. They seem hallowed from that association, and intended naturally to represent pure, tender and devoted thoughts and feelings."[10] As late as 1882, Mrs. M. L. Rayne included a chapter called "The Language of Flowers" in *Gems of Deportment*, an etiquette manual:

> *Flowers have their language. Theirs is an oratory that speaks in perfumed silence, and there is tenderness and passion, and even the light-heartedness of mirth, in the variegated beauty of their vocabulary. No spoken word can approach the delicacy of sentiment to be inferred from a flower seasonably offered. The softest*

How oft doth an emblem but silently tell ∾

sprechen, or speaking through flowers, became a proverb that meant "any flowery or poetic expression with a hidden significance or a message of love."[9]

Madame Charlotte de la Tour, a pseudonym for a French writer, is reputed to have assembled the first floral dictionary in book form. Extant copies are generally undated, but the earliest editions were published around 1820. *Le Langage des Fleurs* was published in the form and size of the small French almanacs so popular with the French women of the time. It was brought to England, translated, and used as the basic source for many of the English and American versions that followed.

Sarah Josepha Hale observed in the introduction to her 1832 edition of *Flora's Interpreter or the American Book of Flowers and Sentiments* (which ran through four-

> *expressions may be thus conveyed without offense, and even profound grief alleviated at a moment when the most tuneful voice would grate harshly on the ear, and when the stricken soul can be soothed only by an unbroken silence.*[11]

Such elegantly bound dictionaries, directed toward an audience of gentle ladies, often provided a plant's Latin name and Linnaean classification, with which the ladies were familiar thanks to their girlhood botany classes. A classical poem was generally featured, making reference to the plant or its symbolism. Often a verse, headed "Sentiment," accompanied a floral gift. Sometimes even an "Answer" was printed, so that a recipient could send a poetic response to the presenter of a certain blossom.

Many flowers' meanings remained constant from volume to volume and era to era. But variations occurred and, occasionally, the sender's intention must have been obscured or confused. The floral language manuals by American Catharine H. Waterman (published in 1852) and Englishman Robert Tyas (1869) both cite the fern as representing "Simplicity," but the former lists the dahlia as meaning "For Ever Thine" and the latter, "My Gratitude Exceeds Your Care."[12] But if there were some discrepancies it hardly mattered; the spirit, enthusiasm, and allure of the exchange could not be dampened. It was a light-hearted pastime.

Mrs. E. W. Wirt, the compiler of the first American language of flowers, in 1829 rhetorically asked in the preface to *Flora's Dictionary:*

Travellers, however, assure us, that the people of the East see something more in them than mere objects of admiration. In the hands of these primitive and interesting people, they become flowers of rhetoric, and speak their feelings with far more tenderness and force than words can impart. With them, there is something sacred in this mode of communication. It is a kind of religious worship—an offering of the fruits of the earth; and, though addressed to an earthly object, it still retains something of the sanctity which belonged to the rite from which it is probably borrowed, and is accompanied with a devotion far more true, and deep, and touching, than the artificial homage which distinguished the courts of Europe, even in the vaunted age of chivalry. . . .

What language could never speak half so well!

Do we make the most of the objects which surround us—do we extract from them all the information, and all the innocent amusement which they are capable of affording? The question is not addressed to the scientific; but to those, of whom the writer admits herself to be one, who are too often content to gaze with a vacant and transient admiration at the works of the creation, and then to remember them no more.

Here, for instance, is this blooming earth: what an interest has the science of botany thrown over it! Yet how few are there, among us, who are disposed to taste of the banquet which this science affords! Again, these flowers interest us by their beauty and fragrance, and here we stop.

What language can convey a compliment so delicate and exquisite? . . . How much easier is it to present a flower, than to make a speech![13]

To provide for year-round pleasure, Mrs. Wirt added, "This mode of communication may be carried even beyond the proper season of flowers, by the aid of an herbarium in which flowers are preserved by simple pressure between the leaves of an album. Such an herbarium would be an ornament to a parlor table, and would, moreover, encourage and facilitate the study of botany."[14]

Collecting treasures from all aspects of the natural world was part of a proper 19th-century education and a primary focus of adults, particularly the "ladies," during leisure

COMMUNICATION THROUGH symbolism was a common
means of expression in the 19th century (preceding pages). From
flowers to women's names, from gems to colors, meaning could be
conveyed in hidden thoughts. To aid in sending coded messages,
many giftbooks were published on specific topics, with the
language-of-flowers books, both in England and America, being
the most popular and pervasive.

TENDER GESTURES BETWEEN women, including the
giving of symbolic flowers, were often portrayed in the fashion
prints of the period. A nosegay, or "tussie mussie," might convey
the wishes of health and happiness. The hand-colored engravings
above are from *Godey's Lady's Book* of 1854 and 1855.

(Jane Ann Allen Album, 1836; Cora Ginsburg Collection)

time. Besides filling herbaria with pressed flowers, exchanging single pressed specimens, and giving fresh or painted flowers, they also exchanged gifts of birds' eggs or gemstones.

Perceived as signifiers of spiritual truths, gemstones have long been objects of symbolism, lore, and superstition. While the more precious stones were generally used for wear and display, modest stones were exchanged in jewelry as tokens of love and affection. The assignment of certain gemstones to represent the signs of the zodiac predates the Roman calendar, and wearing one's birthstone is still considered good luck. The gift of a birthstone to a friend or lover is meant to insure the solidity of the relationship and mutual well-being—and to be a constant reminder of shared warmth. The colors of gems grew to have symbolic meaning as well, and they were often chosen purely for their sparkling hues (for example, blue for constancy and red for passion).

> I bring thee a casket of jewels fair,
> They were culled from the ocean, earth and air,
> In your golden tresses they may not shine,
> But gather them all for your spirit's shrine.
> They are gems from the boundless mine of thought!
> With patience and skill into beauty wrought!
> I have hallowed them all with a prayer for thee,
> Then take them—memorial sweet of me!
>
> —MISS H. J. WOODMAN
> The Language of Gems[15]

Given names have often been chosen for their representative meanings and historical associations. In gift giving, particularly among women, the giver and the recipient's names often inspired the nature of the gift. For instance,

Mary means "The Exalted One," with the apple blossom as her emblem; Elizabeth means faithfulness with the emblem of the blue violet.

Symbols were often exchanged in the form of jewelry, as well as on valentines and friendship cards. It is commonly accepted that an apple presented to a teacher denotes preference, a heart connotes the source of the soul, a horseshoe means good luck, and a loaf of bread is a wish for prosperity. It is perhaps less well known that the gift of a basket signifies the wealth and riches of the maternal body, the butterfly suggests the flight of the soul, and an interlocked chain indicates communication.

Meaningful emblems were also powerful subjects for gravestone art and memorial pieces. These can be contrary to symbols in general usage, as their representations evolved in specific relation to the passage of the soul into the afterlife. Besides being etched onto gravestones, they were printed on paper ephemera to be exchanged and preserved at the time of the loss of a loved one, and found on memorial cards and the borders of postmortem photographs. An anchor represents hope; a clock, the passage of time; a dove, purity or peace.

To the 19th-century romantic, flowers and objects were filled with symbolic meaning, often derived from age-old customs. An acorn drawn in an album suggested that from a small beginning great things could be expected. A shell, which is linked with the necessity of water and its abundance, offered a wish of prosperity. To celebrate a new infant, to acknowledge friendship and love, or even to mourn a death, the symbolism of plants, flowers, birds, animals, and objects appeared on needlework pieces, jewelry, or gravestones.

(M. E. Peabody Album, 1879; Joseph A. Dermont Collection)

Comfort in Mourning

A haunting and prevalent image from the late 18th and 19th centuries is that of a woman, forehead clasped in her hands, leaning on a gravestone in the presence of the symbolic urn that holds the ashes of the departed soul. She is the essence of sorrow. The woman is occasionally joined by her children or husband but more often she stands alone, the sole bearer of grief. While her posture indicates deep suffering, close inspection reveals a powerful strength in her bearing. ¶ Left alone and deeply saddened, the woman still functions. Finely dressed, in either widow's weeds or idealized attire of Grecian style, she is far from pathetic; a female Atlas, she bears a world of grief on her slim shoulders. She is an affirmation of the endurance and fortitude garnered in times of loss. This image of a grieving woman, varied in style and sophistication but not in intent, is found on silk needlework pictures, samplers, porcelains, metalwork, wallpaper, engravings, and jewelry of the period. Women were the creators of the needlework pictures and samplers; their work reflects the way they saw themselves. ¶ Most mothers lost children, many siblings lost siblings, women became widows, young mothers died in childbirth, and all women lost friends. Death, the "King of Terrors,"[1] stalked each home at every social level, and very few families escaped frequent loss. Until the end of the first quarter of the 19th century, America was a rural country. Members of a community participated in their neighbors'

rites of passage, from birth to death, according to their position or skills. In concentrated centers of population, people had similar religious beliefs, values, and cultural standards. They nurtured their own; care of the sick, insane, and impoverished was a communal responsibility. When a member of the community died, whether infant or adult, it affected everyone. Elaborate rituals and funerary practices evolved to enable people to cope with the loss.

By the mid-19th century medical advances and improved sanitation laws significantly decreased the mortality rate, especially of children. The industrial revolution had created new wealth and a new urban and rural middle class. This new group emulated the upper class in funeral etiquette, fashion, and display in an attempt to further separate themselves from the growing lower class. A person's position in society demanded certain behavior in times of grief. Mourning was expected; it was a public demonstration of respect for the dead that followed elaborate dictates of protocol for fashion and behavior. In an effort to avoid a faux pas, etiquette manuals were assiduously studied, and the women's magazines published readers' questions—with answers—on how to interpret the rules.

This attitude trickled down to the lower class who spent precious money on funeral clubs, mourning attire, services, and memorials that often put them in debt for life. Many artifacts created in this culture still survive, representing a preoccupation with death and with memorializing

Mourning memorabilia, all strictly defined within established rules of etiquette, incorporated memorial cards, stationery, fans, handkerchiefs, and mourning pins (pages 174-175). Giftbooks of condolence include self-published volumes that praised the lost loved one's character and deeds. The shimmering silk needlework picture (page 177) is a memorial to two twin sisters. (18¼ × 13"; Private Collection. Photograph courtesy M. Finkel and Daughter) In the photograph opposite, Estelle Carnrite Comstock holds her twin sons, one living and one dead from measles. (1898, American; 4¼ × 6½"; Patricia Comstock Wilczak Collection)

the dead. Needlework, clothing, mourning texts, material printed by mourning warehouses, and etiquette books provide a storehouse of study on these practices.

While American customs never reached the extremes of state, royal, or even upper-class funerals of Europe, those were the role models. Another influence was Queen Victoria herself, but perhaps she is given more credit—or blame—than she is due, as excessive mourning practices were already routine when her beloved consort, Albert, died in 1861. At his passing the devastated Queen was 42 and the mother of nine children. Sequestered at Osborne House, on the Isle of Wight, she and her children made memorial pieces to Albert's memory, and she commissioned many others. Handkerchiefs were embroidered with tears. A photograph of him in his casket was pinned over the Queen's bed, where she slept with his nightshirt in her arms and a cast of his hand close enough for her to reach. She ordered his clothes laid out and hot water prepared each evening, as though he would take his bath. The family was photographed around his bust. By remaining in deep mourning for 40 years, until her own death in 1901, the "Widow of Windsor" reinforced in her dress, attitude, and behavior the socially correct role of widows.

As with so many of the customs of the 19th century, mourning was deeply influenced by the Christian religion. Death was a passage, not a permanent condition; loved ones were not parted forever. All would be joined again in

*I*N THE TABLEAUX VIVANT below, the scene set up to
be photographed shows a woman comforting a friend in mourning.
*(Hand-colored stereograph, circa 1860, American; 7 × 3 ½"; Jan and
Eugene R. Groves Collection)*

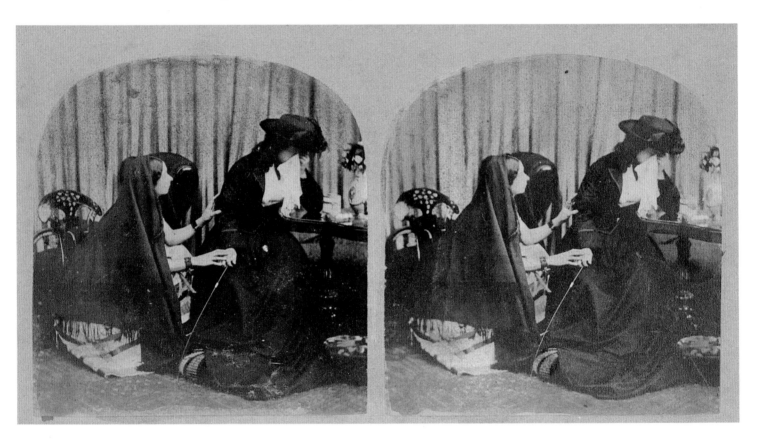

*T*HE COMBINATION OF the poignant postmortems and the
dignity of the women in mourning (overleaf) presents a powerful
image of the way 19th-century Americans faced death. *(Daguerreotypes of mothers holding their babies, child holding flower, deceased
woman, and two women in mourning: Rod MacKensie Collection;
woman in mourning joined with woman in oval frame: Barbara Rusch
Collection; the remainder: Patricia Comstock Wilzcak Collection.)*

heaven after crossing the "mystic river."[2] The mourners also grieved for themselves, as they were left behind.

Traditionally, the women of the family and community provided for family members and friends when illness or death struck. A hierarchy of women caregivers formed an ever widening circle, a ripple effect of relatives, friends, and professionals who ministered to the ill, including the practice of herbal remedies. At births, a midwife stood at the center, while other women assisted her by preparing water, cloths, and other necessities for the procedure, as well as dispensing the food for both family and caretakers.

Martha Ballard, a late 18th- and early 19th-century midwife, eloquently described this cycle of caring in diaries, where she carefully documented her work. In 1793 she acted at 53 births; sometimes more than one occurred in a day. On December 7 she wrote, "At Whites. His wife was delivered at 12 O Clok of a daughter and I was Calld back to Mr. Parkers. His Lady was delivered at 9 hour 30 minutes of a daughter. I am some fatagud."[3] In another entry, she refers to the help of other women: "Mrss. Goffs illness increast & shee was safe delivered at 11 hour 7 30 minute morn of a daughter. Her marm, Mrs Bullin, Mrs Ney were my assistants. Mrs Jacson Came back at 1 h p.m."[4] And when death came, as it did over and over, women like Martha Ballard and her "assistants," those immediate next of kin, attended to the bodies and dressed them in their grave clothes, performing the "last ofice of friendship."[5] They were the "layers out of the dead,"[6] correctly preparing the deceased for burial.

Training young girls for these responsibilities occurred at home or at the home of a relative or friend. Custom held that many young girls "lived out" for a period, learning the ways of homemaking and nursing from women other than their own mothers. Lucy Larcum, in her memoirs of the late 1830s and early 1840s, recalled:

A young woman would have been considered a very inefficient being who could not make and mend and wash and iron her own clothing, and get three regular meals and clear them away every day, besides keeping the house tidy, and doing any other needed neighborly service, such as sitting all night by a sick-bed. To be 'a good watcher' was considered one of the most important of womanly attainments. People who lived side by side exchanged such services without waiting to be asked, and they seemed to be happiest of whom such kindnesses were most expected.[7]

Through this education and experience of caregiving, young girls grew to understand the importance of a woman's role and friendship in times of stress or sorrow. Convinced that they would not be alone when trouble arrived, they wrote of the value of that assurance in their albums:

> *The choicest gift of Heaven is a friend*
> *In whom we confidently may depend*
> *Who'll ease the burden from the throbbing breast*
> *And dull the troubled heart to tranquil rest.*
>
> *May such a friend attend you on through life*
> *And be your guide, and guard you free from strife.*
> *And ever ready to give relief*
> *To mingle joy with joy and grief with grief.*
>
> —FLORA W. GOWER
> MINOT, JANUARY 20TH 1839
> Elizabeth W. Chase Album, 1838-1839

Women knew that, while life would be difficult, there was a powerful, invisible band of strength, women shoulder to shoulder, that surrounded them should they need it. It was the breakdown of these small communities, as relatives

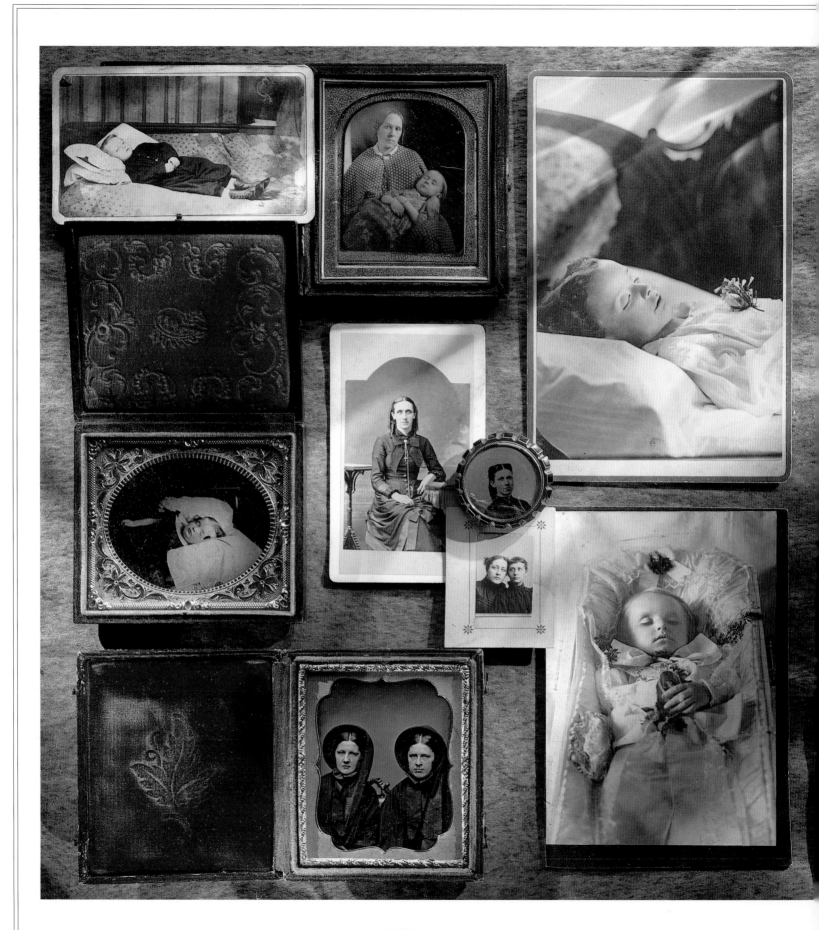

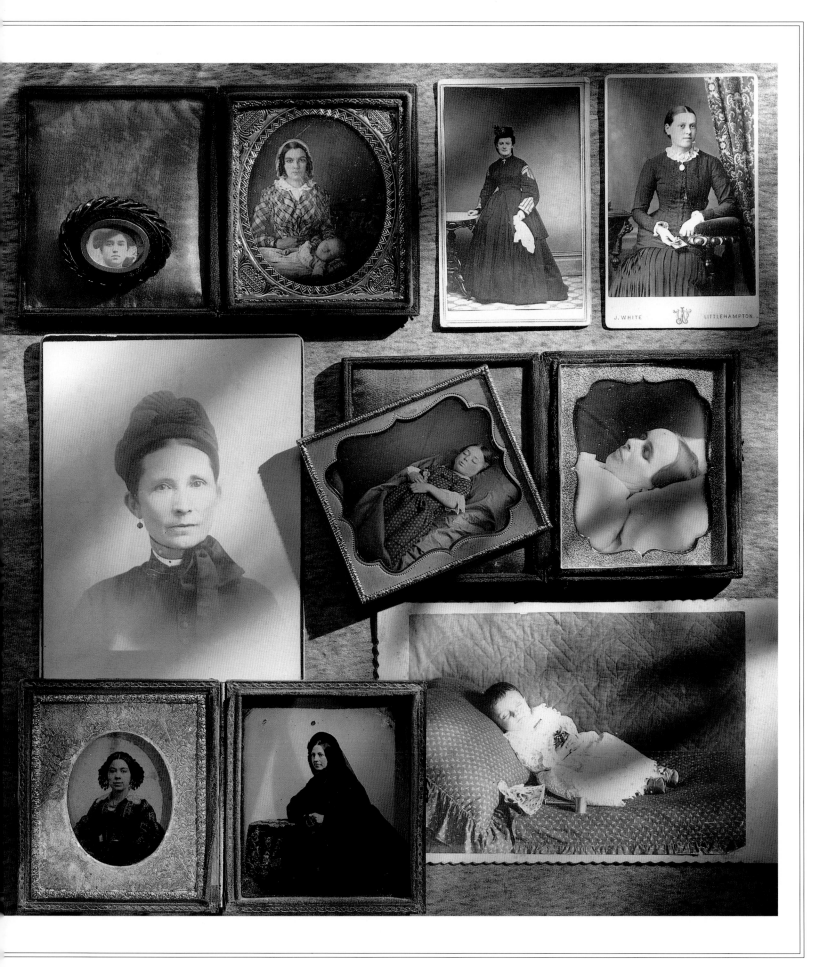

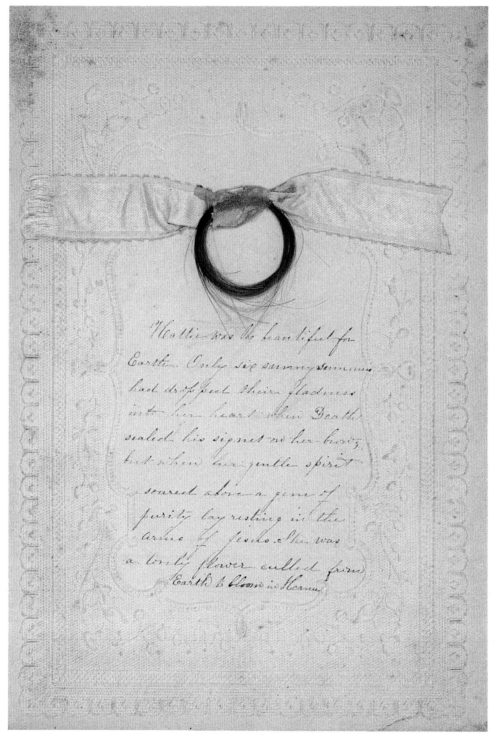

(Circa 1850, American; 4¾ × 7¾")

moved to cities or to the West, that tore apart many women's circles of support. In the 1840s and 1850s references to separation appeared in their albums and letters.

Feb. 1, 1848.

Rain all day. This day my dear husband, my last remaining friend, died.

Feb. 2, 1848.

Today we buried my earthly companion. Now I know what none but widows know; that is, how comfortless is that of a widow's life, especially when left in a strange land, without money or friends, and the care of seven children. Cloudy.

—MRS. ELIZABETH DIXON GEER SMITH, Diary Written on the Oregon Trail, 1847-1848[8]

For widows, economic pressures often created the most immediate problems. Many lost their homes and were separated from their children after all efforts to make a living were exhausted.

For the upper classes, social pressures were more trying than financial concerns. Mourning attire had been worn in America since the colonists had first arrived. Distinction of dress created a barrier, a wall that protected the mourner from facing society and society from dealing with the emotional demands of the mourner. The absolute length of time, as defined by social etiquette, was what built the wall into a prison. Some women were ready to reemerge into society long before custom allowed; and some women today wish that a period of deep grief were more permissible.

Mourning dress and fashion went hand in hand. The signals of mourning were defined to a large degree by both color and texture of fabric. Black was the predominant color, particularly when grieving for adults, but white was also worn by young women or to indicate grief for children. The addition of white to the costume also marked certain stages of mourning. Fashion magazines presented the latest styles, including accessories from black-edged handkerchiefs to parasols.

For men, the etiquette of mourning was less severe, sometimes requiring only bands on hats; the width of the bands indicated the closeness of the relative or the length of time in mourning. Even if it was a man's relative who had passed on, his wife was the one who had to separate herself from society for the appropriate period of time. A widow's mourning was the longest—more than two years, made up of one year of deep mourning followed by stages of "slighting the mourning" and "half mourning." (Half mourning colors were gray, lavender, mauve, and violet). All of the widow's dress and activities were regimented within the strictures of mourning codes, from the jewelry she could wear to the exact size of the black borders on her stationery. The mourning period for a child's or parent's death was one year; for a sister or brother, six months. Lesser time periods were specified for more distant relatives.

The etiquette of mourning created big business, calling for undertakers and funeral homes, hearses and elaborate caskets, mourning warehouses for the sale of clothing, and printed memorial cards and other tokens of friendship. Publishers produced giftbooks specifically to comfort mourners. Friendship albums provide a record of many women's feelings about the mourning process. Within Julia Van Dusen's well-used album, amidst the poetry, prose, and paintings created by her friends, she recorded the joys and sadnesses of her life from 1829 to 1861. She entered a poem to the memory of her child, and on the page she attached the baby's curl:

A Mother is gazing on a lock of hair
  The only relic of a dead child

Thee to whom belonged this hair,
  He the young the sweet the fair,
  He hath vanished into air
And must no more caress me

Could he to this world of pain
  Venture new without a stain
  Ought I wish him back again
To cheet, to soothe, to bless me

Surely, t'would be pasing sweet
  And my heart begins to beat
  At the thought that I might meet
And clasp him once maternally

But O God it must not be
  Keep him, keep him, still from me
  Till Thou take me up to Thee
To dwell with him Eternally.

Julia Van Dusen Album, 1829-1861
(Virginia Makis Collection)

To Julia

Alas my Orphan Sister
You'll not recall the face
Whose meek and lovely likeness
These treasured lines retrace

Oh be like her my own sister
But less in face than mind
I would you could remember
One so tender and so kind.

And keep their gentle monitor
And when you kneel in prayer
Deem an angel's eye is on you
That your Mother watches there

Oh weep that angel mother
Such tears are not in vain
Yet dry them in the hope love
We all shall meet again.

–THELMA K. SHERWOOD
CAZENOVIA, OCT 31ST 1845
Julia Van Dusen Album, 1829-1861
(Virginia Makis Collection)

An earlier entry in the album suggests that Julia lost more than one child. Entitled "lines to the memory of an only child," it expresses the grief that must be borne alone; even friendship cannot salve the pain.

In that same album, 16 years after the first entry, Julia's sister wrote a poem, a consolation piece, to her "Orphan Sister" as they had just lost their mother. The heartfelt poem underscores the value placed on written comfort, which can be called upon repeatedly as the years go by. Letters must have been written too, but it was easier for these single leaves to be lost. What remains in abundance are expressions of sympathy, recorded in albums:

Memorializing the image of a dead loved one, particularly a child, was a common custom. Before the invention of photography and continuing well into the 1860s, "posthumous mourning portraits,"[9] in which the deceased was painted as though still alive, were commissioned. After the invention of the daguerreotype, these paintings could be reproduced so that other relatives or friends might have copies. Painters came into homes to make the paintings, a practice afforded mainly by the well-to-do. Often the painter would make sketches of the deceased and then complete the painting in the studio. The family provided the painter with as many aids as possible, and some members might even stand in for the portrait. Widely known painters such as Raphaelle Peale, Thomas Cole, William Sidney Mount, and Ralph E. W. Early, practiced this art, if somewhat reluctantly, along with many lesser-known painters. It was a profitable business in great demand.[10]

Contemplating the posthumous mourning portrait was part of the ritual of mourning. The artist represented the deceased as alive and in his or her habitual environment. But there was usually a symbol of death—sometimes disguised, sometimes identifiable—in the painting.[11] For example, a child might be portrayed with a lamb, or a young woman, with a lily.

Lydia H. Sigourney, mourning the loss of a friend, reflected on the difficulty of the painter's task and wrote a poem dedicated to the "Artist Sketching the Dead":

Ye weep, and it is well! ~ For tears befit earth's parting.

How still and fair!
  'Tis Beautiful to trace
  Those chisel'd features. Blessed gift is thine

Oh Artist! thus to foil the grave, and keep
  A copy of our jewels, when it steals
  And locks them from us.[12]

After the invention of the daguerreotype in 1839, postmortem photographs—those poignant, direct documents of the deceased—became part of mourning memorabilia, another aid in the grieving process. Unlike the painter with his brush, the photographer's technique could not make the deceased appear alive, but recorded the look of death with accuracy. People came to accept this look and, as the process became less expensive later in the century, the mid-

dle class and even the poor could retain images of their departed loved ones. Sometimes relatives took the body to a photographer's studio, but more often the photographer came to the home to immortalize the deceased in familiar surroundings. The living participated in the documentation process; mothers and fathers posed with their dead children, and siblings posed with dead siblings.

Early postmortem photographs of adults showed only the head and shoulders, often in profile. Children, whose small bodies fit in the camera's frame, might be photographed propped up on a chair, laid out on a settee, or on a bed or in a carriage. The children often held flowers and appeared to be gently sleeping. These little ones, the lambs and angels of the period literature, were frequently buried in the white of purity and innocence.

In early daguerreotypes and ambrotypes, little of the surrounding room was visible. But as techniques advanced, a photographer was able to stand at a greater distance and include the funeral scene. By the 1880s, the atmosphere was portrayed with full casket, flowers, and wreaths.

Sometimes the postmortem photograph was the only one ever taken of a person in his or her life. It would be hung in the parlor, where it had been taken, often encircled by a memorial tribute made of hairwork, wreaths of wax flowers, or needlework. Photographs were also worn in lockets or brooches, frequently combined with strands of the deceased's hair. The jewelry was often engraved with the name of the deceased and the dates of birth and passing.

Victorians were collectors, and even their tears of grief were gathered in specially shaped vials. They believed objects were laden with sentiment and symbolism, and messages could be sent through the choice of a fitting gift.

Lines to the Memory of an Only Child

I ask not even friendship's power

'Tis tears alone that soothe my pain:

That cannot stifle memory's hour,

That cannot give thee back again.

Julia Van Dusen Album, 1829-1861
(Virginia Makis Collection)

Gloves, which were also given as love tokens, were sent to relatives and friends as invitations to a funeral. Their quality varied depending on the economic position of the family. Black silk scarves, black-edged silk handkerchiefs, or black hat bands (also varying in fabric quality) were given as funeral memorials and were in great demand. The well-to-do commissioned memorial rings bearing appropriate symbols of death to give to select funeral celebrants. Some of the symbols used on such jewelry—and on gravestones—included the anchor to mean hope; the clock for the passage of time; the lamb for innocence; the dove or the lily for purity; the palm for victory; violets for humility; the weeping willow for earthly sorrow.[13]

In her album, Caroline Traver pasted obituaries of some of the women in her life.[14] References to faith and fortitude abound. Of Mrs. Rachel Gildersleeve, age 45, "She endured her sickness without complaint, and died in full confidence of salvation through Jesus Christ." Of Martha Ann Case, 34-year-old wife of Reverend William Case, "although called from earth and friends suddenly and unexpectedly, she was found by the Messenger with 'lamp trimmed and burning;' and in the full triumphs of Christian faith she bade earth and friends adieu." Caroline copied into her album, that on "April 12th, 1856, Catherine

Jane Waltermire met her last change with composure and Christian resignation.[15] Many friendship albums include such clipped obituaries.

Phoebe Ann Nichols began her friendship album in 1837. A rich book, it includes entries from her sister, friends, relatives, and daughter. In 1903, after her own death, an unnamed relative entered several poems of consolation, dedicated to her memory:

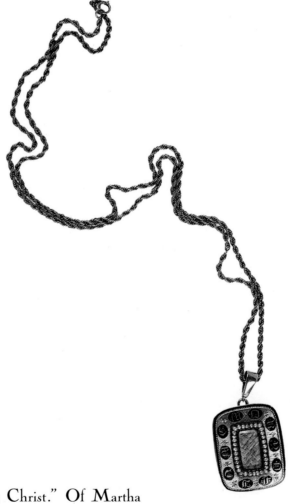

Read at her funeral,
March 27, 1903

Oh do not be discouraged
For Jesus is your friend,
And if you lack for knowlege
He'll not refuse to lend.

Neither will he upbraid you
Though oft times you request.
He'll give you grace to conquer
And take you home to rest.

Phoebe Ann Drew Nichols
Born May 11, 1819
Died March 23, 1903

Phoebe Ann Drew Nichols Album,
1837–1901
(Virginia Makis Collection)

*F*or those confronted with loss in the 19th century, there was an intricate system for expressing grief. Although it may appear excessive, particularly in its dictates of fashion and etiquette, it afforded some a solace that sometimes seems missing in the 20th century.

MARBLE "BOOKS," tokens given by the funeral director
to the family, were often engraved with the initials or name of
the deceased (page 189). Memorial cards would have been given
as a remembrance to friends. A woman in mourning might have
worn the bonnet, scarf, necklace, mourning bag, and lavender
handkerchief shown. The painted wood finial is from a funeral
hearse; the teacup, from a set of mourning china; and the glass vial
is a bottle for saving tears. *(Patricia Comstock Wilczak Collection)*

THE TITLE OF the hand-colored engraving above, "The
Widow's Hope," reflects the psychological and economic reliance
of 19th-century women on men, even, as in this case, a young
male child. *(Jane Ann Allen Album, 1836, English; 4½ × 6½";
Cora Ginsburg Collection)* The mourning locket opposite is engraved
on the reverse side, "Mary Ann Lamb, Died Oct. 30 1856."
(Joe and Honey Freedman Collection)

THE POEM OPPOSITE, from a page of an album, was penned to the memory of a friend by Hannah W. Mekeel in 1841. *(Patricia Comstock Wilczak Collection)*

THE DELICATE, HANDMADE mourning piece above was created to the memory of Maria Newton, deceased December 19, 1823, aged 18 years and six months. It folds, like a purse, into three parts; one contains her lock of hair. *(American; 2¾ × 8¾")*

Stanzas on the death of a Friend.

"Thou art gone to the grave, but we will not deplore thee,
 Though Sorrows, and darkness encompass the tomb;
Thy Saviour has passed through its portall before thee,
 And the lamp of his love is thy guide through the gloom.

Thou art gone to the grave; we no longer behold thee,
 Nor tread the rough paths of this world by thy side,
But, the wide arms of Mercy are spread to enfold thee,
 And sinners may die, for The Sinless has died.

Thou art gone to the grave, and its mansions forsaking,
 Perchance thy weak spirit through fear lingered long;
But the mild rays of Paradise beamed on thy waking,
 And the sound which thou heard was the Seraphim's Song.

Thou art gone to the grave, but we will not deplore thee,
 Whose God was thy ransom, thy guardian, and guide;
He gave thee, He took thee, and He will restore thee,
 And death has no sting, for the Saviour has died."—

Hannah W. Mekeel.

Hector 12th mo 29th 1841.

FORGET ME NOT

Appendix

The Language and Sentiment of Plants, Flowers, Herbs and Trees[1]

FLOWER	INTERPRETATION	FLOWER	INTERPRETATION
Almond	Hope	Hydrangea	Heartlessness
Amaranth, Globe	Unchangeable	Iris	My Compliments
Amaryllis	Beautiful, but Timid	Ivy	Wedded love, Friendship
American Starwort	Welcome to a Stranger	Jasmine, White	Amiability
Anemone	Anticipation	Jasmine, Yellow	Grace and Elegance
Arbor-vitae	Unchanging Friendship	Jonquil	I desire a return of Affection
Bachelor's Button	Hope in Love	Lady's Slipper	Capricious Beauty
Balm	Social Intercourse	Larkspur, double-flowered	Haughtiness
Bay Wreath	Glory	Larkspur, single-flowered	Fickleness
Box	Constancy	Laurel, Mountain	Ambition
Butter Cup	Riches	Lavender	Acknowledgement
Calla	Magnificent Beauty	Lemon Blossom	Discretion
Camellia	Unpretending Excellence	Lily, Scarlet	High-souled
Canterbury Bell	Gratitude	Lily, White	Purity and Beauty
Carnation	Pride and Beauty	Lily, Yellow	Playful Gaiety
Cedar	Think of Me	Lily of the Valley	Delicate Simplicity
China Aster	Love of Variety	Lupine	Dejection, Sorrow
Columbine	Desertion	Magnolia	Love of Nature
Coreopsis	Always Cheerful	Marigold, Yellow	Sacred Affections
Cowslip	Winning Grace	Mignonette	Worth and Loveliness
Crocus	Youthful Gladness	Monk's-hood	Deceit
Cypress	Despair	Moss	Ennui
Daffodil	Uncertainty	Myrtle	Love in Absence
Dahlia	Elegance and Dignity	Narcissus	Egotism and Self-love
Daisy	Beauty and Innocence	Nasturtium	Patriotism
Dandelion	Coquetry	Oak Leaf	Bravery and Humanity
Elder	Compassion	Oats	Music
Everlasting	Always Remembered	Olive	Peace
Fir	Time	Orange Blossom	Woman's Worth
Flax	Domestic Industry	Pansy	Tender and pleasant Thoughts
Forget-me-not	True love	Passion Flower	Religious Fervor
Geranium	Gentility, true Friendship	Peach Blossom	I am your Captive
Goldenrod	Encouragement	Peony	Anger
Hawthorn	Hope	Periwinkle, Blue	Early Friendship
Heart's Ease	Love in Idleness	Periwinkle, White or Red	Pleasures of Memory
Heliotrope	Devotion	Phlox	Unanimity
Holly	Domestic Happiness	Pine	Pity, Immortality
Hollyhock	Ambition	Pink, Red	Woman's Love
Honeysuckle, Coral	Fidelity	Pink, White	Fair and fascinating
Honeysuckle, Wild	Inconstancy	Poppy, Red	Evanescent Pleasure
Hyacinth, Blue	Constancy	Poppy, Scarlet	Fantastic extravagance
Hyacinth, Purple	Sorrow	Poppy, White	Forgetfulness or Consolation

FLOWER	INTERPRETATION
Primrose	Have Confidence in me
Rose, Bridal	Happy Love
Rose, Burgundy	Simplicity and Beauty
Rose, Damask (white and red)	Youth
Rose, Deep Red	Bashful Shame
Rose, Moss	Superior Merit
Rose, White	Sadness
Rose, Yellow	Let us forget
Rosebud, Moss	Confession
Rosebud, Red	Pure and Lovely
Rosebud, White	Too young to Love
Rosemary	Remembrance
Saffron	Marriage
Sage	Domestic Virtues
Snowdrop	Friendship in Adversity
Sorrel, Wild	Parental Affection
Star of Bethlehem	Reconciliation
Sunflower, Dwarf	Your devout Adorer
Sunflower, Tall	Lofty and pure Thoughts
Sweetbrier	Simplicity

FLOWER	INTERPRETATION
Sweet Pea	Departure
Sweet William	A Smile
Thistle, Common	Misanthropy
Thyme	Thriftiness
Tuberose	I have seen a lovely Girl
Tulip, Red	A Declaration of Love
Tulip, Variegated	Beautiful Eyes
Verbena	Fame
Violet, Blue	Faithfulness
Violet, White	Modesty
Virgin's Bower	Filial Love
Wall Flower	Fidelity in Misfortune
Water Lily, White	Purity of Heart
Wheat	Prosperity
Willow, Weeping	Forsaken Lover
Witch Hazel	A Spell
Woodbine	Fraternal Love
Wood Sorrel	Maternal tenderness
Yarrow	Cure for the Heartache
Yew	Penitence
Zinnia	Absence

Language of Ladies Names [2]

NAME	SIGNIFICATION	EMBLEM
Abigail	Father's Joy	Wild Sorrel
Adelaide	Princess	Cardinal Flower
Agnes	Modesty	White Violet
Alberta	All Bright	Pyrus Japonica
Alice, Alicia	Noble	Scarlet Lily
Amanda	To Send Away	Privet
Amelia	Friendship	Box
Amy	A Friend	Ivy
Ann, Anna	Gracious, Giving	Bonus Henricus
Arabella	Fair Altar	Red Tulip
Augusta	Grandeur	Dahlia
Barbara	Welcome to a stranger	American Starwort
Beatrice	One who blesses	Snowdrop
Bertha	Daughter of the Lord	Rush
Betsey, Bessy	Blessed	Everlasting
Beulah	Married	Saffron
Blanche	Fair	Gillyflower
Candice	Contrition	Yew
Caroline	Brave, Valiant	Oak Leaf
Cassandra	Forseeing	Holly
Charlotte	Valiant, Spirited	Hepatica
Chloe	Solace in Adversity	Evergreen Thorn
Christina	Christ's Messenger	Iris
Clara	Clear, Bright	White Pink

NAME	SIGNIFICATION	EMBLEM
Clementine	Mild-tempered	Clematis
Constance	Constancy	Blue Hyacinth
Cornelia	Enduring	Cornelian Cherry Tree
Cynthia	Chaste, Delicate	Lily of the Valley
Daphne	A Laurel	Laurel
Deborah	A Bee	Broomcorn
Delia	Brave	Nasturtium
Diana	Luminous, Splendor	Superb Lily
Dorothy	Gift of God, a Token	Laurustinus
Edith	Happy	Bridal rose
Eleanor	Fruitful, Prosperous	Wheat
Elizabeth	Faithfulness	Blue Violet
Ella	Valor, Strength	Fennel
Ellen	Strong, Worth beyond Beauty	Alyssum
Emily	Beloved	Rosebud
Emma	Loved One	Peruvian Heliotrope
Esther	Secret, Reserved	Maple
Eunice	Good Victory	Bay
Eva	Always cheerful	Coreopsis
Flora	Goddess of Flowers	Rose Geranium
Florence	Flourishing, rich	Buttercup
Frances, Fanny	Frankness	Single White Pink

NAME	SIGNIFICATION	EMBLEM
Georgia	Love of Rural Life	Tulip Tree
Geraldine	Perfect good will	Sweet-scented Tussilage
Gertrude	True to her trust	Sage
Grace	Good will, desire to please	Mezereon
Hannah	Merciful, Charity	Grape
Harriet	Rich Lady	Sumac
Henrietta	Richness, Plenty	Maize
Irene	A Watcher, Activity	Thyme
Jane, Joan	Spiritual Beauty	Cherry Blossom
Jenny	Song Bird, Thankfulness	Agrimony
Josephine	Jasper, Ornament	Hornbeam
Julia	Simplicity, Beauty	Burgundy Rose
Laura	Crowned with laurels Reward of Virtue	A Garland
Louisa, Louise	Surpassing, Worth and Loveliness	Mignonette
Lucinda	Light, Radiant	Ranunculus
Lucy	Light, My Heart is Joyful	Cape Jasmine
Mabel	Lovely, Amiable	White Jasmine
Marcia	Polite, Gentle	Geranium
Margaret	A Pearl, Woman's Worth	Orange Flower
Maria	Full of Grace	Multiflora Rose
Martha	Becoming bitter	Citron
Mary	Exalted, Great and Good	Apple Blossom
Matilda	I'll remember Thee	Rosemary

NAME	SIGNIFICATION	EMBLEM
Melissa	A Bee, Sweetness	Tuberose
Mildred	Mild in Counsel, Sweet Disposition	Mallow
Miranda	Surprise	Truffle
Miriam	Bitterness of Affliction	Weeping Willow
Myra	Sadness	Cypress
Nancy	Gracious, Merciful, Compassion	Elder
Olivia	Peace	Olive
Paulina	Little	Thyme
Phebe, Phoebe	Shining, Genius, Pure	Plane Tree
Priscilla	Ancient	Meadow Saffron
Rachel	A Sheep, Innocence	Daisy
Rebecca	Reconciliation	Star of Bethlehem
Rhoda	Beauty and Prosperity	Red Rose
Rosamond	Rose of the World, Pure and Lovely	Red Rose Bud
Ruth	Contentment	Houstonia
Sarah	Princess, Elevation	Fir Tree
Sibyl	Foretelling	Oleander
Sophia	Wisdom	Red Mulberry
Susan	A Lily, Purity and Modesty	White Lily
Susanna	Joy	Wood Sorrel
Tabitha	Clear Sighted, Beautiful Eyes	Tulip
Victoria	Victory	Palm Tree

Natal Stones and Flowers of the Months[3]

MONTH	GEM	FLOWER
January	Garnet	Snowdrop
February	Amethyst	Primrose
March	Jasper, Blood Stone	Violet
April	Diamond, Sapphire	Daisy
May	Emerald	Hawthorn
June	Agate	Honeysuckle
July	Turquoise	Water-lily
August	Carnelian	Poppy
September	Chrysolite	Morning-glory
October	Beryl	Hops
November	Topaz	Chrysanthemum
December	Ruby	Holly

Gemstone Color Language[4]

GEMSTONE COLOR	MEANING
White	Life, innocence, joy, pleasure
Blue	Constancy, virtue, truth, heaven
Red	Love, fire, passion, emotion
Green	Hope, victory
Purple	Suffering, sorrow, regal
Yellow	Goodness, faith

Symbolism of Objects[5]

OBJECT	MEANING	OBJECT	MEANING
Acorn	Great Effort Leading to Great Achievement	Garland	Bonding
Almond	Sweetness, Hope of Heaven	Gold	The Sun, Riches, Wealth
Amber	Tears, Courage	Grapes	Fertility
Amulet	Protection from Danger or Death	Halo	Supernatural Force
Anchor	Hope, Salvation	Hand, Single	Support
Angel	Heavenly Guardian, Protector, Ministering Spirit, Messenger	Harp, Lyre	Dispels Evil Spirits, Bridge between Heaven and Earth
Apple	A Means to Immortality, Fruitfulness, a Love Charm	Heart	The Center, the Source of Love, the Center of the Soul
Arch	Purity	Honey	Wisdom
Arrow	The Male	Horseshoe	Good Luck
Basket	The Maternal Body	Hummingbird	Love Charm
Bee	Secret Knowledge, Industry, Diligence, Wealth	Key	Mystery, Opener of Knowledge
Bell	Fertility charm, Protection from Evil, Creative Power	Knot	Linkage, Bonding, Connections without Beginning or End
Birch	Safeguard against Wounds or Evil	Lamb	Purity, Innocence
Bird	Warning, Advice, Prophecy, the Human Soul	Lamp	Intelligence, Spirit
Boat	The Cradle, the Mother's Womb	Loaves of Bread	Fecundity, Prosperity
Book	Knowledge	Lyre	Union
Bow	God's Power	Mask	Mystery, Secrecy
Box	A Feminine Symbol, a Receptacle	Mirror	Imagination, Thought, Self Contemplation
Butterfly	The Soul	Moon	Creation and Recreation of the Universe, the Cycles of Woman
Candle, Lighted	Individual Light or Life	Necklace	A Cosmic Symbol of Ties and Bonds, Unity, Continuity
Cat	The Moon, Guardian of Marriage	Old Man, Woman	The Past, Wisdom
Chain	Bonds, Communication	Owl	Wisdom
Chestnut	Curative powers	Peacock	Vanity
Child	The Future	Plait, Braid	Intimate Relationship, Interdependence
Circle	Heaven, Perfection	Pomegranate	Oneness
Clasped Hands	"Hands in Trust Forever," The Bonds of Friendship	Ribbons knotted together like a Garland	Immortality, Crowning, Fulfillment
Clover, Three-Leafed, Trefoil	Trinity	Ring	Wholeness, Continuity
Clover, Four-Leafed	Good Luck	Scales	Justice
Cock	Sun, Vigilance, Activity	Ship	Joy, Happiness
Cornucopia	Abundance	Silver	The Moon, the Feminine Form
Cricket	Personification of the House Spirit, Conveyor of Good Luck	Star	The Spirit
Crown	Preeminence, Royalty	Sun	Heroism
Dove	Soul	Swan	Satisfaction of Desire, Immaculate Whiteness
Eagle	Height of Spirit, National Emblem	Torch	Purification through Illumination
Egg	Immortality	Tree	Life
Fan	Phases of the Moon	Unicorn	Chastity
Feather	The Wind, Faith, Contemplation	Whippoorwill	Return to a Special Place, Wish come True
Fish	Unconscious, the Spirit, Fertility	Wings	Spirituality, Imagination, Thought
Fleur-de-lis	Royalty	Wren	Good luck

Serpent = Eternity

The Language of Gems[6]

GEM	SENTIMENT	GEM	SENTIMENT
Agate	Long Life, Health, and Constancy	Jasper	Pride of Strength
Amazon Stone, Feldspar	Friendship, Good Wishes	Jet	Sad Remembrance
Amber	Disdain	Lapis Lazuli	Nobility
Amethyst	Peace of Mind	Moonstone	Pensive Beauty
Aquamarine	Hope	Natrolite	Female Friendship
Beryl	Forget-me-not	Obsidian	Mutual Amity, Thy Smile is My Sunlight
Bloodstone	Farewell, I mourn your absence		
Carnelian Onyx	Distinction Lies before Thee	Onyx	Reciprocal Love
Cat Sapphire	Affability, Power	Opal	Pure Thoughts
Cat's Eye	Platonic Love	Pearl	Modest Loveliness
Coral	Thy Choicest Jewel is Thy Heart	Rose Quartz	Remembered in Prayer
Cornaline	Thou Art Formed to Guide, True Greatness	Ruby	Courage and Success in Dangerous and Hazardous Enterprise
Cornelian	Friendship in Sorrow	Sapphire	Innocence
Diamond	Forever Thine, True Love	Topaz	Fidelity
Emerald	Success in Love	Tourmaline	Generosity
Fire Opal	Adversity Cannot Crush Thee, Energy	Turquoise	The Most Brilliant Success and Happiness in Life, Fortune Favors Thee
Garnet	Fidelity in Every Engagement, Virtue		
Jade	Remembrance	Zircon	Respect

Footnotes

Presentation page: *Keepsake of Friendship*, ed. G. S. Monroe (Boston: Phillips, Sampson & Company, 1854). Title page: Raphael Tuck Valentine, circa 1880; Nancy Rosin Collection.

CHAPTER 1
The Handwritten Word

1. Charles Francis Potter in *Funk & Wagnalls Standard Dictionary of Folklore, Mythology and Legend,* ed. Maria Leach (New York: Funk & Wagnalls Company, 1949), pp. 94-95.

2. Ibid., p. 95.

3. Ibid.

4. John Carter, *ABC for Book Collectors* (New York: Alfred A. Knopf, 1991), p. 100. A book's format signifies the number of times the printed sheet was folded into leaves. In the folio size, the sheet was folded once, in quarto, twice, and in octavo, three times. Thus, the size is a half, a quarter, and an eighth of the original sheet, respectively.

5. Leach, p. 95.

6. Louisa Henrietta Sheridan, ed., *The Comic Offering; or Ladies' Melange of Literary Mirth for 1831* (London: Smith, Elder and Co., 1831), p. 259.

7. Ibid.

8. *Real Pen Work: Self Instructor in Penmanship* (Pittsfield, MA: Knowles and Maxin, 1881).

9. Mrs. C. W. Denison, *Godey's Lady's Book and Magazine* (Philadelphia: Louis A. Godey, Publisher, January 1856): p. 55.

10. Carol F. Karlsen and Laurie Crumpacker, eds., *The Journal of Esther Edwards Burr 1754-1757* (New Haven: Yale University Press, 1984), pp. 50-51.

11. Ibid., p. 53.

12. C. Vann Woodward, ed., *Mary Chesnut's Civil War* (New Haven: Yale University Press, 1981), p. 724.

13. Blanche Benniarde, "To Laura and the Album," *Peterson's Ladies National Magazine,* vol. XXVII, no. 4 (Philadelphia: April 1855): p. 289.

Quote, p. 26: Alma Lutz, *Emma Willard: Daughter of Democracy* (Boston: Houghton Mifflin Company, 1929), p. 49. Emma Willard was one of the most important figures in the advancement of higher education for women in 19th-century America. Illustration: M. A. B. English Album, circa 1833; Jutta Buck Collection.

Illustrations p. 29 (left to right): Sarah Ann Gedney Album, 1827-1844, Helen Walvoord Collection; Rebecca Jackman Album, 1846-1849, Virginia Makis Collection; Mary Haviland Album, 1859-1860, Helen Walvoord Collection; Jane Ann Allen Album, 1836, Cora Ginsburg Collection.

Horizontal quote, pp. 34-35: Abigail B. Clark, Milford, May 14, 1845, in Mary C. Curtis Brown Album, 1811-1852 (Brown University Library).

CHAPTER 2

Printed Pages of Sentiment

1. Ralph Thompson, ed., *American Literary Annuals and Gift Books* (Archon Books, 1967), p. 3.

2. Frederick W. Faxton, *Literary Annuals and Gift Books* (Private Libraries Association, 1973), p. viii.

3. *The Album* (New York: F & R Lockwood, 1824), dedication page.

4. E. L., "The Souvenir," in *Affection's Gift* (1882, p. 55), as quoted in *American Literary Annuals and Gift Books,* ed. Ralph Thompson (Archon Books, 1967) p. 2.

5. Today the word "miniature" is technically used in the book dealer/collector world for a book under three inches in size, but in the 1840s it was used for giftbooks of this size, often with the word "miniature" as part of the title.

6. Henry W. Herbert, ed., *The Magnolia* (New York: A. & C. B. Edwards, 1841), p. 3.

7. Alistair Allen & Joan Hoverstadt, *The History of Printed Scraps* (London: New Cavendish Books, 1990), p. 9.

8. Thompson, p. 13.

9. The following list of editors is far from exhaustive; likewise the titles of the annuals they edited are merely a representative sampling: Harry F. Anners (*The Gift of Friendship, The Hyacinth, The Remember Me*); Samuel G. Goodrich, who also used the name Peter Parley (*The Token, The Moss Rose*); Reynell Coates (*Leaflets of Memory*); Rufus W. Griswold (*Gift of Love*); N. P. Willis (*The Token*). A number of women edited several titles—even in one year. In America, a few of the better-known editors were Sarah Josepha Hale, who was the influential editor of *Godey's Lady's Book* for 40 years (*Flora's Interpreter, The Opal*); Clara Arnold (*The Magnolia*); Miss Sarah C. Edgarton (*The Rose of Sharon*); Mrs. Emeline P. Howard (*The Moss Rose*); Miss Eliza Leslie (*The Gift, The Violet*), Mrs. M. A. Livermore (*The Lily of the Valley*); Caroline May (*The Woodbine*); Mrs. Frances S. Osgood (*The Floral Offering*); Mrs. Emily Percival (*The Amaranth, Gems of Beauty, The Diadem*); Mrs. Lydia H. Sigourney (*The Christian Keepsake, The Religious Souvenir*); and Miss Catharine Waterman (*Flora's Lexicon, Friendship's Offering, The Religious Offering*).

10. Thompson, pp. 21-22.

11. *The Album,* p. 34.

12. Thompson, p. 23.

13. Douglas Ball, *Victorian Publisher's Bindings* (Williamsburg, VA: The Book Press, 1985), p. 3.

14. Rev. S. D. Burchard, ed., *The Laurel Wreath* (New York: Leavitt & Allen, circa 1856), pp. 9-13.

Quote, p. 59: J. M. Fletcher, ed., *The Golden Gift, A Token for All Seasons* (Boston: J. Buffum and Co., 1853), p. 46. Illustration: H. C. Album, 1824-1855, English, Helen Walvoord Collection.

CHAPTER 3

Collections Between Covers

1. Charles Kingsley, "Glacus, or The Wonders of the Shore" (Cambridge, 1855), as quoted in *The Heyday of Natural History 1820-1870,* ed. Lynn Barber (Garden City, NY: Doubleday & Company, 1980), p. 125.

2. Peter Bayne, "Life and Letters of Hugh Miller" as quoted in *The Heyday of Natural History 1820-1870,* p. 134.

3. *Art Recreations: Being a Complete Guide* (Boston: J. E. Tilton, 1860), p. 259.

4. *The Young Lady's Book: A Manual of Elegant Recreations, Exercises and Pursuits* (London: Whitehead and Compy, 1838), pp. 85, 115, 61.

5. Ibid., p. 85.

6. Shirley Hibberd, *The Fern Garden: How to Make, keep and Enjoy It or, Fern Culture Made Easy* (London: Groombridge and Sons, 1881), p.3.

7. *Art Recreations: Being A Complete Guide,* p. 292.

8. *Art Recreations: Being A Complete Guide,* p. 292.

9. Eva Marie Niles, *Fancy Work Recreations: A Complete Guide to Knitting, Crochet, and Home Adornment* (Minneapolis: Buckeye Publishing Co., 1885), p. 275.

10. *Art Recreations: Being A Complete Guide,* p. 292.

11. Harlan H. Ballard and S. Proctor Thayer, *The American Plant-Book for the Convenient Preservation and Analysis of Pressed Flowers, Ferns, Leaves and Grasses* (New York: Daniel Slote & Co., 1879), introduction.

12. H. B. Anson , *Leaf and Flower Pictures, and How to Make Them* (New York: D. F. Randolph, 1857), pp. 38-39.

13. The Nancy Rosin Collection.

14. Anson, pp. 39-40.

15. Leslie Hyde, *The Diaries of Sally and Pamela Brown 1832-1838,* ed. Gertrude Elaine Baker and Blanche Brown Bryant (1887; reprint, Springfield, Vermont: The William L. Bryant Foundation, 1979), p. 7.

Horizontal quote, p. 65: Moss Album, 1863.

Illustration, p. 66: Rebecca Beach Judson Herbarium, 1840, American, Robert Fraker Collection.

Illustration, p. 72: M. Y., circa 1833, English Album, Jutta Buck Collection.

CHAPTER 4

Tokens from the Heart

1. A Lady, *Young Lady's Friend* (Boston, American Stationers Society, 1836), p. 279.

2. Ruth E. Finley, *Old Patchwork Quilts and the Women Who Made Them* (Philadelphia: J. B. Lippencott Company, 1929), p. 95.

3. Ibid, p. 191.

4. Carrie A. Hall and Rose G. Kretsinger, *Romance of the Patchwork Quilt in America* (Caldwell, ID: The Caxton Printers, Ltd., 1936), p. 17.

5. Finley, p. 191.

6. Susan Burrows Swan, *Plain and Fancy American Women and Their Needlework, 1700-1850* (New York: Holt, Rinehart and Winston, 1977), p. 205.

7. Ruth Webb Lee, *A History of Valentines* (Wellesley Hills, MA: Lee Publications, 1952), p. 5.

8. Ibid., p. 8.

9. Ibid., p. 14.

Illustration, p. 87: unsigned, circa 1833, English Album, Jutta Buck Collection.

Illustration, p. 95: J. Leigh, H. C. Album, 1824-1855, English, Helen Walvoord Collection.

Illustration, p. 103: Hannah Crawford Renwick Fern Album, n.d., English, Nancy Rosin Collection.

CHAPTER 5

The Lasting Memento

1. C. Vann Woodward, ed., *Mary Chesnut's Civil War* (New Haven: Yale University Press, 1981), p. 285.

2. Mrs. C. S. Jones and Henry T. Williams, *Ladies' Fancy Work: Hints and Helps to Home Taste and Recreations* (New York: Henry T. Williams, 1876), p. 52.

3. J. B. Syme, ed., *The Mourner's Friend or Sighs of Sympathy for Those Who Sorrow* (Worcester: S.A. Howland, 1852; Patricia Comstock Wilczak Collection), p. 74.

4. Katharine Morrison McClinton, *Collecting American Victorian Antiques* (New York: Charles Scribner's Sons, 1966), p. 259.

5. Jones and Williams, p. 49.

Horizontal quote, pp. 112-113: Joe and Honey Freedman Collection.

CHAPTER 6

Exchange of Likenesses

1. Hannah R. London, *Miniatures and Silhouettes of Early American Jews* (Rutland, VT: Charles E. Tuttle Company, 1970), p. 6.

2. Betsey Creekmore, *Traditional American Crafts* (Hearthside Press, Inc., 1968), p. 122.

3. London, p. 49.

4. Ruth Hayden, *Mrs. Delany: Her Life and Her Flowers* (London: Colonade Books, British Museum Publications Ltd., 1980), pp. 65, 115, 165.

5. Alan Trachtenberg, ed., *Classic Essays on Photography* (New Haven: Leete's Island Books, 1980), p. 29.

6. Alma Davenport, *The History of Photography: An Overview* (Boston: Focal Press, 1991), p. xiii.

7. Trachtenberg, p. 37.

8. Trachtenberg, p. 38.

9. Trachtenberg, p. 38.

10. "Canadian Women's Studies," vol. 2, no. 3 (1980, p. 7), in *Camera Finds & Kodak Girls: 50 Selections by and about Women in Photography, 1840-1930,* ed. Peter E. Palmquist (New York: Mid March Arts Press, 1989), p. 11.

11. Trachtenberg, p. 40.

12. Trachtenberg, p. 41.

13. Stefan Richter, *The Art of the Daguerreotype* (New York: Viking Press, 1989), pp. 14-15.

14. Ibid., p. 5.

15. Davenport, p. 19.

16. Davenport, p. 19.

17. Davenport, p. 20.

18. A. Bogardus, *Century Magazine,* vol. 68 (1), no. 89 (1904), in *Cartes de Visite in Nineteenth Century Photography,* by William C. Darrah (Gettysburg, PA: W. C. Darrow, 1981), p. 24.

19. Ibid, p. 22.

Horizontal quote, p. 131: "The Album of Carte de visite and Cabinet Portrait Photographs" (London: Reedminister Publications Ltd., 1974) in *The Photographic Experience,* curated by Heinz K. and Bridget A. Henisch, The Palmer Museum of Art, Pennsylvania State University, University Park, PA: 1988, p. 8.

Quote, p. 128: Martha Cameron, *Peterson's Ladies' National Magazine,* volume XXV, no. 2 (Philadelphia, 1854): p. 37.

CHAPTER 7

To My Teacher

1. Ethelda Coggin papers, 5 August 1853, Alfred P. Malpa Ephemera Collection.

2. Lucy Larcom, *A New England Girlhood Outlined From Memory* (1889; reprint, Williamstown, MA: Corner House Publishers, 1985), p. 44.

3. Betty Ring, *American Needlework Treasures: Samplers and Silk Embroideries from the collection of Betty Ring* (New York: E. P. Dutton, 1987), p. 8.

4. Ibid., p. 40.

5. Ethel Stanwood Bolton and Eva Johnston Coe, *American Samplers* (New York: Dover Publications, 1973), p. 370.

6. Ibid., p. 265.

7. Ibid., p. 266.

8. Alice Morse Earle, ed., *The Diary of Anna Green Winslow, A Boston School Girl of 1771* (1894; reprint, Williamstown, MA: Corner House Publishers, 1974), p. 34.

9. *Art Recreations: Being A Complete Guide* (Boston: J. E. Tilton and Company, 1860), pp. 145-148.

10. Earle, p. 48.

11. *A Girl's Life Eighty Years Ago: Selections from the Letters of Eliza Southgate Browne* (1887; reprint, Williamstown, MA: Corner House Publishers, 1980), p. 17.

12. *Harriet Rider Album, 1835-1864,* Nancy Rosin Collection.

13. Larcom, pp. 167-170.

14. Larcom, pp. 170-175.

15. "Young Ladies Portfolio," October 1858.

16. Larcom, p. 157.

17. Larcom, pp. 267-269.

Horizontal quote, p. 153: Bolton and Coe, p. 265.

CHAPTER 8

Hidden Languages

1. Robert Tyas, "Romance of Nature," in *The Language of Flowers or Floral Emblems of Thoughts, Feelings and Sentiments* (London: George Routledge and Sons, 1869), pp. vi-vii.

2. Mrs. S. J. Hale, *Flora's Interpreter: or the American Book of Flowers and Sentiments* (Boston: Marsh, Capen & Lyon, 1832), title page.

3. Ernst and Johanna Lehner, *Folklore and Symbolism of Flowers, Plants and Trees* (New York: Tudor Publishing Company, 1960), p. 109.

4. Hale, p. 2.

5. *The Letters and Works of Lady Mary Wortley Montagu,* "edited by her Great Grandson, Lord Wharncliffe", vol. 1 (Paris: Baudry's European Library, 1837), p. 5.

6. Ibid., pp. 286-287.

7. Mrs. Almira H. Lincoln, *Familiar Lectures on Botany, Practical, Elementary and Physiological, with an Appendix, Containing Descriptions of The Plants of the United States and Exotics, &c.* (New York: F. J. Huntington & Co., 1840), p. 14.

8. *A Correct Dictionary of Flowers,* "compiled by The Most Talented Authors," n. d., p. 1.

9. Lehner, p. 109.

10. Hale, p. iii.

11. Mrs. M. L. Rayne, *Gems of Deportment and Hints of Etiquette* (Detroit: Tyler & Co. 1882), p. 320.

12. Catharine H. Waterman, *Flora's Lexicon: An Interpretation of the Language and Sentiment of Flowers: with an Outline of Botany, and a Poetical Introduction* (Boston: Phillips, Sampson and Company, 1852), pp. 83, 73; Robert Tyas, pp. 87, 66.

13. Mrs. E. W. Wirt of Virginia, *Flora's Dictionary* (Baltimore: Fielding Lucas, Jr. 1829), p. 3.

14. Ibid., p. 4.

15. Miss H. J. Woodman, *The Language of Gems with Their Poetic Sentiments* (Boston: Tompkins and B. B. Mussey, 1851), p. 5.

Quote, p. 165: Waterman.

Horizontal quote, pp. 166-167: Robert Tyas, *The Language of Flowers or Floral Emblems of Thoughts, Feelings, and Sentiments* (London: George Routledge and Sons, n.d.), title page.

CHAPTER 9
Comfort in Mourning

1. *Caroline E. Traver Album, 1852-1868,* Tobias Ricciardelli Collection.
2. Ibid.
3. Laurel Thatcher Ulrich, *A Midwife's Tale: The Life of Martha Ballard, Based on Her Diary, 1785-1812* (New York: Vintage Books, 1991), p. 165.
4. Ibid., p. 103.
5. Ibid., p. 47.
6. Martha V. Pike and Janice Gray Armstrong, *A Time to Mourn: Expressions of Grief in Nineteenth Century America* (Stony Brook, NY: The Museums at Stony Brook, 1980), p. 15.
7. Lucy Larcom, *A New England Girlhood Outlined from Memory* (1889; reprint, Williamstown, MA: Corner House Publishers, 1985), pp. 190-191.
8. Mirra Bank, *Anonymous Was a Woman* (New York: St. Martin's Press, 1979) p. 102.
9. Pike and Armstrong, p. 71. A term used by Phoebe Lloyd in her essay "Posthumous Mourning Portraiture."
10. Ibid., pp. 71-73.
11. Ibid., p. 73.
12. Mrs. L. H. Sigourney, "The Weeping Willow" (Hartford: Henry S. Parsons, 1847; Anchor and Dolphin Collection) p. 49.
13. Barbara Jones, *Design for Death* (New York: Bobbs-Merrill, Co. Inc., 1967), p. 229; Duval and Higby, eds., Early American Gravestone Art (New York: Dover Publications, 1978), p. 132.
14. Traver Album, Ricciardelli Collection.
15. Ibid.

Horizontal quote, p. 187: J. B. Syme, ed., *The Mourner's Friend, or Sighs of Sympathy for Those Who Sorrow* (Worcester: S. A. Howland, 1852), p. 9.

APPENDIX

Illustration, p. 195: Sarah Ann Gedney Album, 1827-1844, American, Helen Walvoord Collection.

1. Adapted from Mrs. S. J. Hale, *Flora's Interpreter: or the American Book of Flowers and Sentiments* (Boston: Marsh, Capen & Lyon, 1832).
2. Adapted from Sarah C. Carter, *Lexicon of Ladies' Names with Their Floral Emblems* (Boston: J. Buffum, 1853).
3. Adapted from George Frederick Kunz, *Natal Stones, Sentiments and Superstitions Associated with Precious Stones* (New York: Tiffany & Co.).
4. Adapted from *The Funk & Wagnalls Standard Dictionary of Folklore Mythology and Legend,* Maria Leach, ed. (New York: Funk & Wagnalls Company, 1949).
5. Ibid.
6. Adapted from Mrs. H. J. Woodman, *The Language of Gems with Their Poetic Sentiments* (Boston: A. Tompkins and B. B. Mussey, 1851).

Bibliography

Alcott, Wm. A. *Letters to a Sister, or Woman's Mission.* Buffalo, NY: Geo. H. Derby and Co., 1850.

Allen, Alistair, and Joan Hoverstadt. *The History of Printed Scraps.* Great Britain: New Cavendish Books, 1990.

Anson, H. B. *Leaf and Flower Pictures, and How to Make Them.* New York: D. F. Randolph, 1857.

Art Recreations: Being a Complete Guide. Boston: J. E. Tilton and Company, 1860.

Ball, Douglas. *Victorian Publisher's Bindings.* Williamsburg, VA: The Book Press, 1985.

Ballard, Harlan H., and S. Proctor Thayer. *The American Plant-Book for the Convenient Preservation and Analysis of Pressed Flowers, Ferns, Leaves and Grasses.* New York: Daniel Slote & Co., 1879.

Bank, Mirra. *Anonymous Was a Woman.* New York: St. Martin's Press, 1979.

Barber, Lynn, ed. *The Heyday of Natural History 1820-1870.* Garden City, NY: Doubleday & Company, Inc., 1980.

The Bazar Book or Decorum: The Care of the Person, Manners, Etiquette, and Ceremonials. New York: Harper & Brothers, 1870.

Bolton, Ethel Stanwood, and Eva Johnston Coe. *American Samplers.* New York: Dover Publications, Inc., 1973.

The Book of Manners: A Guide to Social Intercourse. New York: Carlton & Phillips, 1852.

Carter, John. *ABC For Book Collectors.* New York: Alfred A. Knopf, 1991.

Chase, Ernest Dudley. *The Romance of Greeting Cards.* Cambridge: Rust Craft Publishers, University Press of Cambridge, 1956.

A Correct Dictionary of Flowers, compiled by "The Most Talented Authors," n.p., n.d.

Creekmore, Betsey B. *Traditional American Crafts.* Hearthside Press, 1968.

Darrah, William C., *Cartes De Visite in Nineteenth Century Photography.* Gettysburg, PA: W.C. Darrah, 1981.

Davenport, Alma. *The History of Photography: An Overview.* Boston: Focal Press, 1991.

Decorum: A Practical Treatise of Etiquette and Dress of the Best American Society. New York: Union Publishing House, 1880.

Duval and Higby. *Early American Gravestone Art.* New York: Dover Publications, 1978.

Earle, Alice Morse, ed. *Child Life In Colonial Times.* 1899. Reprint. Williamstown, MA: Corner House Publishers, 1989.

Earle, Alice Morse, ed. *The Diary of Anna Green Winslow, A Boston School Girl of 1771.* 1894. Reprint. Williamstown, MA: Corner House Publishers, 1974.

Emery, Sarah Anna. *Reminiscences of a Nonagenarian.* Newburyport, MA: William H. Huse & Co., 1879.

Faxton, Frederick W. *Literary Annuals and Gift Books.* Private Libraries Association, 1973.

Finley, Ruth E. *Old Patchwork Quilts and the Women Who Made Them.* Philadelphia, PA: J. B. Lippencott Company, 1929.

Fisher, Laura. "A Quilt Goes Home, 1887 Documentary Textile Winds Its Way Back to Lynn, Massachusetts." N.p., 1989.

Gernsheim, Helmut, and Alison Gernsheim. *The History of Photography from the Camera Obscura to the Beginning of the Modern Era.* New York: McGraw-Hill Book Co., 1969.

A Girl's Life Eighty Years Ago: Selections from the Letters of Eliza Southgate Browne. 1887. Reprint. Williamstown, MA: Corner House Publishers, 1980.

Gregg, John. *The American Chesterfield, or Way to Wealth, Honor and Distinction; Being Selected* from the Letters of Lord Chesterfield to His Son; and Extracts From *Other Eminent Authors, on the Subject of Politeness with Alterations and Additions, Suited to the Youth of the United States.* Philadelphia, 1828.

Hall, Carrie A., and Rose G. Kertsinger. *The Romance of the Patchwork Quilt in America.* Caldwell, Idaho: The Caxton Printers, LTC, 1936.

Hartley, Miss Florence. *The Ladies' Hand Book of Fancy and Ornamental Work, Comprising Directions and Patterns.* Philadelphia: G. G. Evans, Publisher, 1859.

Hayden, Ruth. *Mrs. Delany: Her Life and Her Flowers.* London: Colonade Books, British Museum Publications Ltd., 1980.

Hersey, Heloise Edwina. *To Girls: A Budget of Letters.* Boston: Small, Maynard & Company, 1901.

Hibberd, Shirley. *The Fern Garden: How to Make Keep and Enjoy It or, Fern Culture Made Easy.* London: Groombridge and Sons, 1881.

Hilliard, Nicholas. *Nicholas Hilliard's Art of Limning.* Boston: Northeastern University Press, 1983.

Hollingsworth, Buckner. *Flower Chronicles.* New Brunswick, NJ: Rutgers University Press, 1958.

Hunt, Gaillard, Litt. D.I. *Life in America One Hundred Years Ago.* Williamstown, MA: Corner House Publishers, 1976.

Hyde, Leslie. *The Diaries of Sally and Pamela Brown 1832-1838.* Bryant, Blanche Brown, and Gertrude Elaine Baker, eds. 1887. Reprint. Springfield, VT: The William L. Bryant Foundation, 1979.

Jones, Barbara. *Design for Death.* New York: Bobbs-Merrill, Co., Inc., 1967.

Jones, Mrs. C. S., and Henry T. Williams. *Ladies' Fancy Work: Hints and Helps to Home Taste and Recreations.* New York: Henry T. Williams, 1876.

Karlsen, Carol F., and Laurie Crumpacker, eds. *The Journal of Esther Edwards Burr 1754-1757.* New Haven: Yale University Press, 1984.

Kolter, Jane Bentley. *Forget Me Not: A Gallery of Friendship and Album Quilts.* Pittstown, NJ: The Main Street Press, 1985.

Kunz, George Frederick. *Natal Stones, Sentiments and Superstitions Associated with Precious Stones.* New York: Tiffany & Co., 1909.

A Lady. *Young Lady's Friend.* Boston: American Stationer's Society, 1836.

Larcom, Lucy. *A New England Girlhood Outlined from Memory.* 1889. Reprint. Williamstown, MA: Corner House Publishers, 1985.

Leach, Maria, ed. *The Funk & Wagnalls Standard Dictionary of Folklore, Mythology and Legend.* New York: Funk & Wagnalls Company, 1949.

Lee, Ruth Webb. *A History of Valentines.* Wellesley Hills, MA: Lee Publications, 1952.

Lehner, Ernst, and Johanna Lehner. *Folklore and Symbolism of Flowers, Plants and Trees.* New York: Tudor Publishing Company, 1960.

The Letters and Works of Lady Mary Wortley Montagu. "Edited by her Great Grandson, Lord Wharncliffe." Paris: Baudry's European Library, 1837.

Lincoln, Mrs. Almira H. *Familiar Lectures on Botany, Practical, Elementary and Physiological, with an Appendix, Containing Descriptions of the Plants of the United States and Exotics &c.* New York: F. J. Huntington & Co., 1840.

London, Hannah. *Miniatures and Silhouettes of Early American Jews.* Rutland, VT: Charles E. Tuttle Company, 1970.

Longford, Elizabeth. *Queen Victoria Born to Succeed.* New York: Harper & Row, Publishers, 1964.

The Lowell: Offering Writings by New England Mill Women (1840-1845). Edited and with an Introduction and Commentary by Benita Eisler. New York: Harper Torchbooks, 1977.

Lutz, Alma. *Emma Willard: Daughter of Democracy.* Boston: Houghton Mifflin Company, 1929.

McClinton, Katharine Morrison. *Collecting American Victorian Antiques.* New York: Charles Scribner's Sons, 1966.

Milford, Humphrey. *Early Victorian England.* Volumes 1 and 2. London: Oxford University Press, 1934.

Moffat, Mary Jane, and Charlotte Painter, eds. *Revelations Diaries of Women.* New York: Vintage Books, 1975.

Morley, John. *Death, Heaven and the Victorians.* Pittsburgh, PA: University of Pittsburgh Press, 1971.

Mrs. Chapone to a Lady. *Letters on the Improvement of the Mind: Addressed to a Lady, by Mrs. Chapone;* Dr. Gregory to his daughters, *A Father's Legacy to His Daughters By Dr. Gregory; Lady Pennington to her absent daughters, A Mother's Advice to Her Absent Daughters, with an Additional Letter on the Management and Education of Infant Children by Lady Pennington,* ed. W. Marks, New York, 1830.

Newhall, Beaumont. *The History of Photography.* New York: The Museum of Modern Art, 1982.

Niles, Eva Marie. Fancy Work Recreations: *A Complete Guide to Knitting, Crochet and Home Adornment.* Minneapolis, MI: Buckeye Publishing Co., 1885.

Palmquist, Peter E., ed. *Camera Finds & Kodak Girls: 50 Selections by and about Women in Photography, 1840-1989.* New York: Mid March Arts Press, 1989.

Pearson, Norman Holmes, ed. *The Complete Novels and Selected Tales of Nathaniel Hawthorne.* New York: The Modern Library, 1937.

Peterson's Ladies National Magazine. Volume XXVII, No. 4. Philadelphia: April 1855.

Peterson's Ladies National Magazine. Volume XXV, No. 2. Philadelphia: 1854.

Pike, Martha V., and Janice Gray Armstrong. *A Time to Mourn: Expressions of Grief in Nineteenth Century America.* Stony Brook, NY: The Museums at Stony Brook, 1980.

Proctor, Molly. *Needlework Tools and Accessories: A Collector's Guide.* London: B. T. Batsford, 1990.

Pullan, Mrs. *The Lady's Manual of Fancy-Work: A Complete Instructor in Every Variety of Ornamental Needle-Work.* N.p.: Dick & Fitzgerald, Publishers, 1859.

Rayne, Mrs. M. L. *Gems of Deportment and Hints of Etiquette*. Detroit: Tyler & Co., 1882.

Real Pen Work: Self Instructor in Penmanship. Pittsfield, MA: Knowles and Maxim, 1881.

Richter, Stefan. *The Art of the Daguerreotype*. New York: Viking, 1989.

Rickards, Maurice. *Collecting Printed Ephemera*. New York: Abbeville Press, 1988.

Ring, Betty. *American Needlework Treasures: Samplers and Silk Embroideries from the Collection of Betty Ring*. New York: E. P. Dutton, 1987.

Sherwood, Mrs. John. *Manners and Social Usage*. New York: Harper and Brothers, 1887.

Spruill, Julia Cherry. *Women's Life and Work in the Southern Colonies*. New York: W. W. Norton & Company, 1972.

Staff, Frank. *The Valentine and Its Origins*. New York: Frederick A. Praeger, 1969.

Swan, Susan Burrows. *Plain and Fancy American Women and Their Needlework, 1700-1850*. New York: Holt, Rinehart and Winston, 1877.

Thompson, Amy Adwyna. *The Examination of the Gift-Books and Annuals in the Harris Collection of Brown University*. Providence, RI: Brown University, 1931.

Thompson, Ralph, ed. *American Literary Annuals and Gift Books*. Archon Books, 1967.

Tompkins, A., and B. B. Mussey. *The Language of Gems with Their Poetic Sentiments*. Boston, 1851.

Trachtenberg, Alan, ed. *Classic Essays on Photography*. New Haven, CT: Leete's Island Books, 1980.

Tyas, Robert. *The Language of Flowers or Floral Emblems of Thoughts, Feelings, and Sentiments*. London: George Routledge and Sons, n.d.

Ulrich, Laura Thatcher. *A Midwife's Tale: The Life of Martha Ballard, Based on Her Diary, 1785-1812*. New York: Vintage Books, 1991.

The Young Lady's Book: A Manual of Elegant Recreations, Exercises and Pursuits. London: Whitehead and Compy, 1838.

Webster, Marie D. *Quilts: Their Story and How to Make them*. New York: Tudor Publishing Company, 1915.

Wehle, Henry B. *American Miniatures 1730-1850*. Garden City, NY: Garden City Publishing Company, Inc., 1837.

Wells, Richard A., A.M. *Manners, Culture and Dress of the Best American Society*. Springfield, MA: King, Richardson & Co., 1891.

Woodward, C. Vann, ed. *Mary Chesnut's Civil War*. New Haven, CT: Yale University Press, 1981.

Young, John H., A.M. *Our Deportment or the Manners, Conduct and Dress of the Most Refined Society; Including Forms for Letters, Etc., Etc. Also Valuable Suggestions on Home Culture and Training*. Springfield, MA: W. C. King & Co., 1882.

Giftbooks and Literary Annuals

The Album. New York: F. & R. Lockwood, 1824.

Anners, Henry F. *The Remember Me: A Token of Love for 1854*. Philadelphia, 1854.

Arnold, Clara, ed. *The Magnolia; or Gift-Book of Friendship*. Boston: Phillips, Sampson & Company, 1854.

Burchard, Rev. S. D., ed. *The Laurel Wreath*. New York: Leavitt & Allen, circa 1856.

Carey and Lea. *The Atlantic Souvenir for 1831*. Philadelphia, 1831.

The Casket: A Gift-Book for All Seasons. New York: Leavitt & Allen, n.d.

Christmas Blossoms and New Year's Wreath for 1847. Boston: Phillips & Sampson, 1847.

Coates, Rayne, M. D., ed. *Leaflets of Memory: An Illuminated Annual for 1851*. Philadelphia: E. H. Butler & Co., 1851.

Coates, Reynell, M. D., ed. *Leaflets of Memory: An Annual for 1844*. Philadelphia: Butler and Williams, 1844.

Colman, Miss, ed. *The Ladies' Vase of Wild Flowers: A Collection of Gems from the Best Authors*. New Orleans: Burnett & Bostwick, 1854.

Denison, Mrs. C. W. *Godey's Lady's Book and Magazine*. Philadelphia: Louis A. Godey, Publisher, 1856.

Doten, Elizabeth, ed. *The Lily of the Valley for 1855*. Boston: James M. Usher, 1855.

Fletcher, J. M., ed. *The Golden Gift: A Token for All Seasons*. Boston: J. Buffum and Co., 1853.

The Forget Me Not: A Gift for All Seasons. New York: Nafis & Cornish, n.d.

Friendship's Offering; and Winter Wreath: A Christmas and New Year's Present for 1836. London: Smith, Elder and Co., 1836.

Friendship's Offering: A Christmas, New Year, and Birthday Gift. New York: Leavitt & Allen, n.d.

Goodrich, S. G., ed. *The Token; or Affection's Gift. A Christmas and New Year's Present*. New York: Leavitt & Allen, n.d.

Goodrich, S. G., ed. *Winter Wreath of Summer Flowers*. New York: D. Appleton and Co., 1854.

Hale, S. J. *Flora's Interpreter, or the American Book of Flowers and Sentiments*. Boston: Marsh, Capen, & Lyon, 1832.

Halpine, Miss Mary G., Rev. C. Stone, and William C. Brown, eds. *The Mother's Assistant and Young Lady's Friend*. Boston: Browne & Halpine, 1854.

Hanson, J. W. *An Offering to Beauty: Composed of the Choicest Descriptions of Female Loveliness, Virtues, Accomplishments, Attractions, and Charms; Comprising the Poetry of Woman*. Lowell, MA: Merrill and Straw, 1853.

Herbert, Henry W., ed. *The Magnolia*. New York: A. & C. B. Edwards, 1841.

Howard, Mrs. Emiline P., ed. *The Moss Rose for 1850*. New York: Nafis and Cornish, 1850.

Kearney, Edward. *The Casket: A Souvenir for 1845*. New York, 1845.

Keese, John, ed. *The Opal: A Pure Gift for the Holydays*. New York: J. C. Rike, n.d.

King, David P. *The Ladies' Gift or Souvenir of Friendship*. Boston, 1851.

The Ladies' Wreath and Parlor Annual. New York: Burdick and Scovill, n.d.

L. E. L.: Longman, Rees, Orme, Brown, Green. *Heath's Book of Beauty*. London, 1833.

Leavitt & Allen. *Juvenile Forget Me Not: A Christmas and New Year's Present*. New York, n.d.

Livermore, Mrs. M. A., ed. *The Lily of the Valley for 1852*. Boston: James M. Usher, 1852.

Longman, Rees, Orme, Brown and Green. *The New Year's Gift and Juvenile Souvenir*. London, 1831.

Martyn, S. T., ed. *The Ladies' Wreath: An Illustrated Annual for 1848-49*. New York: Martyn & Ely, 1848-1849.

Martyn, S. T., ed. *The Ladies' Wreath: An Illustrated Annual for all Seasons*. New York: J. M. Fletcher & Co., 1852.

Monroe, G. S., ed. *The Keepsake of Friendship: A Christmas and New Year's Annual for 1853*. Boston: Phillips, Sampson & Company, 1853.

Monroe, G. S., ed. *The Keepsake of Friendship: A Christmas and New Year's Annual for 1854*. Boston: Phillips, Sampson & Company, 1854.

Monroe, G. S., ed. *The Keepsake of Friendship: A Christmas and New Year's Annual for 1855.* Boston: Phillips, Sampson & Company, 1855.

The Mother's and Young Lady's Annual: A Gift Book for the Holidays. Boston: Cyrus Stone, Publishers, 1853.

Osgood, Frances S. *The Floral Offering: A Token of Friendship.* Philadelphia: Carey and Hart, 1847.

Percival, Emily, ed. *The Garland or Token of Friendship: A Christmas and New Year's Gift for 1852.* Boston: Phillips, Sampson and Company, 1852.

Percival, Emily, ed. *The Amaranth or Token of Remembrance: A Christmas and New Year's Gift for 1855.* Boston: Phillips, Sampson, and Company, 1855.

Percival, Emily, ed. *The Golden Gift: A Wreath of Gems from the Prose and Poetical Writers of England and America. Prepared Especially as a Gift Book for All Seasons.* Boston: Phillips, Sampson, and Company, 1853.

Percival, M. J., ed. *The Oasis or Golden Leaves of Friendship.* Boston: Wentworth & Co., 1856, 1847.

Percival, Francis E., ed. *Sweet Home, or Friend-ship's Golden Altar.* Boston: L. P. Crown & Co., 1856.

Percival, Walter, ed. *The Lady's Gift: A Souvenir for All Seasons.* Nashua, NH: Charles T. Gill, 1849.

Phillips, Alfred A, ed. *The Forget Me Not for 1849.* New York: Nafis and Cornish, 1849.

Reynolds, Frederic Mansel, ed. *The Keepsake for 1830.* London: Chance and Co., 1830.

Ritchie, Leitch. *Friendship's Offering of Sentiment and Mirth.* London: Smith, Elder and Co., 1844.

Sheridan, Louise Henrietta, ed. *The Comic Offering; or Ladies' Melange of Literary Mirth for 1831.* London: Smith, Elder, and Co., 1831.

Sigourney, Mrs. L. H. "The Weeping Willow." Hartford: Henry S. Parsons, 1847. Anchor and Dolphin Books Collection.

Sigourney, Mrs. L. H., and others. *The Young Ladies' Offering; or Gems of Prose and Poetry.* Boston: Phillips and Sampson, 1848.

Syme, J. B., ed. *The Mourner's Friend, or Sighs of Sympathy for Those Who Sorrow.* Worcester, MA: S. A. Howland, 1852. Patricia Comstock Wilczak Collection.

Thayer, Mrs. J., ed. *The Golden Present: A Gift for All Seasons.* Nashua, N.H.: J. Buffum and Co., 1850.

The Token of Friendship: An Offering for All Seasons. Boston: Phillips, Sampson and Company, n.d.

A Token of Remembrance. D. Appleton & Co., n.d.

Waterman, Catharine H. *Flora's Lexicon: an Interpretation of the Language and Sentiment of Flowers with an Outline of Botany, and a Poetical Introduction.* Boston: Phillips, Sampson and Company, 1852.

Wirt, Mrs. E. W. *Flora's Dictionary.* Baltimore: Fielding Lucas, Jr., 1829.

Woodman, Miss H. J. *The Language of Gems with Their Poetic Sentiments.* Boston: A. Tompkins and B. B. Mussey, 1851.

Author's Note: I have included miniature giftbooks and *Language-of-Flowers* books in this category. While they do not strictly belong to the giftbook genre, as they were not edited and published annually, both were given in the same context as the giftbooks and literary annuals.

Index

Page numbers in *italics* refer to illustrations.

African-Americans, 54
Album(s), 8, 12-13, 84, 108; American, 29, 31, *32-33, 34*; autograph, 44; commercial, 31; dedication of, 40; floral, 62, 71, *158-159, 160, 167*; hair, *106-107*, 108, *109*, 110-113, *114, 115, 116, 117*; house, *76, 77*; memory bouquet, *70-71, 71*; monogram, 77; photographic, 127, *129*, 133; schoolgirl, 8, 28, *152-153*; scrap, 72, 77, *78-79*; size of, 31; specimen, *60-61*, 62-72, *63, 68. See also* Friendship Album.
Album amoricum, 25, 29
Album box, portfolio style, *21, 25*, 31
Almanacs, 50; French, *49, 166*
Ambrotype, 127, 131-132, 187

Annuals, 50, 52, 54, 57
Art, schoolgirl, *140-141, 143*, 151
Artists, American, 51
Autograph, books, 44; writers, 41

Beadwork, 92, *93*
Bell jars, 12, 60, 64
Berlin Work, 89, *90-91*, 92
Bookplates, 56
Botany, 166; study of, 64, *164, 167*
Browning, Elizabeth Barrett, 130

Calotype, 127
Camera obscura, 124
Cards: cabinet, 127, 133; calling, 14, *55*, 77, *90-91*, 92, 95, 99-100; friendship, *18-19*, 85, 94, 172; greeting, 76; memorial, 185, 191; trade, 76, *77*; visiting, 132
Carte de visite, 127, 132, *132*
Chromolithography, die-cut, 72, 100; invention of, 51, *77*; title pages, 53
Collodion, use of, in photography, 131-132
Commonplace book, 12, 25, *77*; defined, 44
Cutwork, 20, *43*, 88; description of, 95. *See also* Scherenschnitten.

Daguerre, Louis-Jaques-Mandé, 126, 127
Daguerreotype, *118-119*, 126, *126*-127; 130-132, *150, 157, 182-183*; daguerreotypists, 130, 132; use of, in memorializing, 186-187. *See also* Photography.

Die cut, processes, 76; scrap, 21, 72, 77, 100, 112
Dry plates, invention of, 131

Engravings: hand-colored, 27, 50, 56, 72, 76, 99, *170, 191*; periodical, 111; steel and copperplate, 31, 51, 52; subject matter of, 51-52, 176

Fern collecting, 62, 64-65
Floral dictionaries, 166-167
Flowers: collecting, 62; decorative, 11, *25*, 31, 100, 166; engravings, 51; memorial, 187; paintings, *15, 72, 75*, 110, *173*; popularity, 164; pressed, 12; symbolism/language of, 14, 51, 52, 92, 95, 102, 158-173, 196-198
Folk art, 110; folk artists, 122
Friendship: importance of, 8, 181, 186; poems, 144, *146*; puzzles, 21, 100; topic of, in giftbooks, 51, 54, 57; in samplers, 145; wreath, 100, *101*, 143. *See also* Quilts, Tokens.
Friendship Album, 8, *9*, 18-45; borrowing, *44*; contents, 20, 35, 44, 64, *75*, 100, 133, 137, 163; hairwork, 110-113; intent, 20, 34; mourning, 185-186, 190; titles, 38, *158-159*
Freundbuch, *25, 31*

Gems, symbolism in, 160, 170, 172
Giftbooks, 46-59; condolence, *174-175*, 185; editors, 52; miniature, 51, *55*; origin, 50; popularity, 48, 52; publishers, 50-52; size, 51; symbolism and, *168-169*; teacher/scholar exchange, 148; tokens and, 12, 84, 112; writers, 52, 54
Gravestones, *176*; symbolism on, *172*, 190

Hair, 106-117; friendship album and, 133; hairwork, *13*, 21, 38, 45, *94*, *106-107*, 108, 110-113, *114, 115, 116, 117*; jewelry and, 102; memorial pieces and, 112, 185, 187, 192; miniatures and, 120, 122; use of, for thread, 88; wreaths, 8, 13, 44. *See also* Album(s), Tokens.
Hale, Sarah Josepha, 8, 11, 54, 166
Heliography, 126
Herbarium (herbaria), 12, 67, 70, 163, 167, 172
Historians, material for, 44, 110
History, women's role in domestic, 8, 12, 111, 145
Hollow cut, 122, *123*, 124

Jewelry: hair art as, 108; miniatures set in, 120; mourning, 124, 176, 185, 187, 190; of sentiments, 12, 102, *104-105*, 172; portraits in,

setting, 133; symbolism in, *104-105*, 172; use of, in daguerreotypes, 131.
Journals, 12, 20, 41, 44, 72, 142, 151

Labels, 76, *109*, 145; linen, 21, 77, 94, 111
Limning, 120

Men: albums carried by, 29; economic reliance on, 13, *191*; entires written by, 8, 40-41; giftbook editors, 52; images carried by, 122; mourning etiquette for, 185
Mourning, 174-193; attire, 185, *189*; etiquette, 178, 185; memorabilia, *174-175*, 187; piece, *192*; portraits, *180, 182-183, 186-187*; religious influence on, 178, 181; subject of, in albums, 22, 51, 54; symbolism and, *172*, 176, 187, 190; texts, 185; tokens, *189*

Native Americans, 54; beadwork, 92, *93*
Nature: album subject, 22, 34, 54; beauty of, recorded, 12, 153; collecting specimens of, *60-61*, 62, 64-65, 67, 167; Romanticism and, 164; theme of, as teacher, 70
Needles, 85, 87, 95, 144-145; needle cases, 84, 87
Needlework, 50, 84; cases, 77; design, 89; mourning and, 178, 187; schoolgirl, 92, 124, 144-145, 151; symbolism in, 172. *See also* Berlin Work, Quilts.
Needlework pictures. *See* Samplers.

Painting: floral, *72, 75*, 110; landscape, 45; nature, 64; Oriental, 35, 151; photography and, 126; Poonah, 35, 151; postmortem, 186; schoolgirl, 124, 151; theorem, *15*, 35, *73*, 151; use of, in albums, *15*, 35, *75*, 110, 185. *See also* Watercolors.
Papyrotamia, 95, 99
Photography, 118-137; invention of, 120, 126-127; mourning and, *172, 182-183*, 186, 187; portraits, *121, 129, 134, 135, 136, 137*; public opinion of, 130; social implications of, 12, 122, 127
Pierced paper, pinprick, 95
Pins, 87, 95; pincushions, 84, 87, 95
Poetry: symbolic gifts and, 163; use of, in albums, 11, 12, 20, *25*, 44, 50, 51, 52, 64, 70, 72, 74, 185; in copybooks, 152; in valentines, 99
Poets: American, 44; English, 29, 44
Poonah painting, 35, 151
Portrait miniatures, 120, 122, *123*, 127
Punchwork, *90-91*, 92

Queen Victoria, 102, 122, 133, 178
Quilts, 12, *86*, 87-89

Remembrancers, 12, 20
Repoussé, 95

Samplers, 12, 89, 144-145, *148, 149*, 176
Scherenschnitten, 95, 99
Scrap, 72, *109*; die-cut, 21, 72, 77, 100, 112
Scrap book, 72, 78-79
Sea moss, 12, 64-65, 67, 68
Selam, *162, 163*-164
Shadow boxes, 12, 64
Shadow portraits, 124
Silhouettes, 120, 122-123
Sketchbooks, 12, 64, 72, 161
St. Valentine, 95, 99
Stammbücher, 31
Stenciling, 35, 151
Symbolism, 158-173, 196-200; animals, 172; communication through, *168-169*; death, 190; gems, 198; gravestone, *172*, 190; hands, 11, *14*, *55*, 102, 163; hearts, 38; jewelry, 102, 172, 190; love, 95; mourning, 187; names, 197-198; plants, *163, 164*, 172; objects, 199-200; religious, 35; urn, 176. *See also* Flowers.

Talbot, William Henry Fox, 124, 127
Teacher, influence of, on scholars, 140-157. *See also* Tokens.
Theorem painting, *15*, 35, *73*, 151
Tintype, 127, *132*, 133
Tokens, 82-105; affection, 12, 20, 108, 190; friendship, 11, 12, 13, 21, 38, 50, *82-83*, 84, 85, *90-91, 92-103, 93, 94, 97, 98, 101*, 102, 114, 122, 185; funeral, *189*, 190; hair, 13, 108, 110-113, *111, 114, 115, 116, 117*, 148; symbolic, 160; teacher/scholar, 142, 144, *146*

Valentines, *32-33*, 41, 76, 77, 84, 85, 95, 98, 99, *172*

Watercolors: cutwork, 95; disappearance of, 44; miniatures, 122; schoolgirl art and, *140-141, 143*, 151; sketchbooks, 72; use of, in albums, *15, 18-19*, 20, 24, 31, *32-33*, 35, 110, 163
Whimsy boxes, 12, *82-83*, 85
Widows, 185
Willard, Emma, 26

Acknowledgments

To my friends and colleagues, my kindred spirits in collecting, a deep thank you. These pages could not have been written, the photographs could not have been made without your willingness to share your treasures, both with me and with the reader. I am deeply grateful for your generosity, your cooperation, your time and efforts, your knowledge, and your friendship:

Elizabeth Baird, Valentines, Portland, ME; George Barlow, Murray Hill Antique Center, New York, NY; Jean Berger; Jutta Buck, Jutta Buck Antiquarian Book & Print Seller, Pine Plains, NY; Patricia Byrne; Joseph A. Dermont, J. & J. Dermont, Bookseller, Onset, MA; Mary Donaldson and Roberta Batt, M.D., Pekl, Portland, ME; Gary Ewer; Bonnie Ferriss, Lake Luzerne, NY; Amy Finkle, M. Finkle and Daughter, Philadelphia, PA; Cecily Barth Firestein; Laura Fisher, Laura Fisher Antique Quilts & Americana, New York, NY; Robert Fraker, Savoy Books, Lanesboro, MA; Joe and Honey Freedman, Merion Station, PA; Harold Gaffin; Cora Ginsburg, Cora Ginsburg, Inc., New York, NY; Carol Greenberg, Cornucopia, Syosset, NY; Jan and Eugene R. Groves, Baton Rouge, LA; Roberta Hansen, Roberta Hansen Art and Antiques, Yarmouth, ME; James A. Hinck and Ann Marie Wall, Anchor & Dolphin Books, Newport, RI; Robin Fake; Tordis Ilg Isselhardt, Images from the Past, Bennington, VT; Drew Heath Johnson; Moira E. Kelly and John Jenner, Kelly & Jenner American Antiques, Sherman, CT; Mona and Marc Klarman; Alice Kozlowski, The Four'um Antiques, Springfield, MA; Evelyn L. Kraus, Ursus Books and Prints, Ltd., New York, NY; Virginia Makis, The Four'um Antiques, Springfield, MA; Alfred P. Malpa, Farmington, CT; Rod MacKenzie; Tobias Ricciardelli, Tobias Ricciardelli Antiques, Stanfordville, NY; Nancy Rosin, Valentines and Love Tokens, Franklin Lakes, NJ; Barbara Rusch; Helen Walvoord; Dennis A. Waters, The Daguerreian Forum, Exeter, NH; Roger and Kristine Williams; Patricia Comstock Wilczak.

Special thanks to Mark N. Brown, Curator of Manuscripts, Brown University Library, Providence, RI.

I am indebted to:

Nancy Lindemeyer, editor of *Victoria* Magazine, whose leadership and intuitions have spurred so many of us to discover forgotten ports of the 19th century;

William Frost Mobley and Emily Davis Mobley, who swept me through the door of The Ephemera Society of America into a world of preservationists working individually and collectively to preserve our fragile paper history;

John Graf of the Daguerreian Society, whose newsletter led me to a network of those conserving the first American photographs;

Michael McLaughlin and Stefan Hagen, my technical assistants, whose expertise, patience, and good humor sustained me through the photography sessions;

Floyd Yearout, my agent, for his long-term support and wise advice through so many of my projects;

Andrew Stewart, for his immediate enthusiasm for this material, his commitment to bring it to a larger audience, and for his gift of the lovely title for this book, and Leslie Stoker, for her belief that many women would want to see the gentle tokens their foremothers had made for each other;

All those at Stewart, Tabori & Chang whose hearts, hands, and hard work contributed to making this book a reality.

My deep appreciation to both Mary Luders, my editor, whose guidance and counsel were invaluable on a day-to-day basis throughout the process of writing this book, and to Lynn Pieroni Fowler, my designer, whose artistic sensitivity to each individual image shaped the pieces into an evocative and elegant whole.

Words of gratitude to those who aided me in this project would be incomplete without a salute to my husband, Donald, and my son, Robin, who offered support and encouragement and who provide the richness of my life. To both of you, my thanks—and love.

— STARR OCKENGA

Design by Lynn Pieroni Fowler

Text set in Nicolas Cochin with Centaur,
composed in-house by Barbara Sturman, on a Macintosh IIsi
with QuarkXpress 3.1, and output on a Linotronic L300 by
Typogram, New York, New York.

Printed and bound by
Tien Wah Press (Pte.), Ltd., Singapore